the art of felt

the art of felt

inspirational designs, textures and surfaces

text and photographs by
Françoise Tellier-Loumagne

Thames & Hudson

Contents

Introduction

This book explains and illustrates the creative techniques that can be used to make felt and felted fabrics, with a stress on close observation of the world around us and in particular, the endless source of inspiration that can be found in the sky. These are the three main textile types described in this book:

• **Wet felting** is done by matting together wool fibres, using moisture, heat and friction. The finished fabric can vary in thickness and suppleness.

• **Needle felting** can be done with both woollen and synthetic materials, which take on a felted appearance on one or both sides.

• **Tufting** is the process of passing threads or yarns through a base fabric to create textured, smooth or felted surfaces.

At home, wet felting can be done by hand or with the aid of a washing machine, while needle felting and tufting can be done using specially designed needles or, more recently, with a specialized machine. The same methods can be used both by beginners and students and by experienced designers and professionals.

Looking to the sky for inspiration

When choosing a basic theme for inspiration, it's important to select one that offers a chance to explore new territory instead of reusing the same techniques again and again, as well as providing a stress-free environment in which to experiment with new ideas.

Here we've chosen to explore the sky. Why? Because in everyday life, it's easy to forget that it's there – especially in the city – but in fact it's always present, always changing, and always breathtaking. It may also seem like a difficult theme at first, but it's surprisingly easy to achieve stunning effects in broad strokes, rather than becoming tangled up in too many small details. There's also less risk of becoming kitsch or corny or out of style.

Why is the sky such a great subject for felting? Well, many yarns and textiles lend themselves easily to cloudy effects, swirling shapes and graduated colours; needle felting and tufting can be highlighted with embroidered details and used to create a range of textures, fluffy and round or smooth and plain, giving a feel of movement, depth and space.

Above all, the projects in this book are designed to make everyone take a fresh look at the world around them and use those ideas for inspiration, innovation and self-expression.

Felting basics

Wet felting

Origins and uses

The origins of felt lie in the distant past: at least 3,000 years ago or probably more. It is difficult to give a precise date because textiles generally do not survive for hundreds of years. If we take into account that mankind has been farming sheep for more than 10,000 years, it could be speculated that feltmaking was discovered relatively soon afterwards. Rugs of felted wool were certainly being made at the time of Attila the Hun (AD 432–453).

In fact, the felting of wool and other animal fibres is based on a natural process. Heat, humidity and friction cause wool fibres to become matted and entangled so that they cannot be separated. All these types of fibre are covered in tiny scales, invisible to the naked eye, which flake and open when all these conditions are present. The higher the temperature, the faster the transformation occurs. Certain products can be added to activate the process, including soap, acids such as vinegar, or soda.

Wool is the easiest material to felt but this can vary considerably depending on the source of the fibre. Nowadays, many commercially available wools

Page 4: Altocumulus clouds with swirling edges.

Pages 6–7: A felted knit fabric and a sky full of scattered clouds: the similarities are striking.

Opposite: Wool fibre, a cloud you can hold in your hand.

are treated to prevent felting. It's therefore important to choose your materials carefully to give your project the best chance of success.

Felt is used widely in industry for its excellent sound and heat insulation properties, and also has many other uses: it is found inside pianos, to make seals and washers, filters and polishing discs. It is extremely hardwearing, difficult to tear, and also porous, hence its use in felt-tip pens and printers, and it can be cut to very precise sizes and thicknesses, almost to the micron. In addition, it does not fray or unravel, so that even lightly felted fabrics such as boiled wool, flannelette and fleece do not require hemming or finishing.

Felt is also widely used in packaging for luxury items such as perfumes and jewelry, in display stands and shelving, in car interiors, in children's toys and as a surface for board games and pool tables. It can be worn in the form of slippers, hats and berets, other fashion items and accessories, or can decorate the home as rugs, cushion covers and throws.

Felt is a non-woven, a type of textile that is increasingly dominant in industry, but its decorative potential is now being explored by a wider public.

Inside a felt factory, tiny wool fibres easily become hooked to any rough surface.

Left: Gathering up wool fibres for recycling.

Right: Wool, the raw material of the feltmaking process.

Industrial wet felting

Generally, industrial felt is not made from pure wool but from a wool/viscose mixture, in the proportions 30 %/70 %, for example. The raw fibres are first mixed together and then carded, which means separating and combing them lengthways, like brushing hair. This produces fine webs of fabric which are layered together in alternating directions to produce what is known as a batt. Its thickness is proportional to the desired thickness of the final felt: a batt 15 cm (6 in.) thick will produce a finished felt 1 mm ($\frac{1}{24}$ in.) thick. The batts are then pressed between the vibrating plates of a hardening machine and steam-treated to moisten them. The damp felt is then fed into a fulling machine to shrink and compress it. This process can take between 30 minutes and 3 hours.

Images from a felt factory in Mouzon, France.
Opposite:
    1 – The raw fibres before the felting process begins.
    2 – Cylinders studded with mechanical teeth are used to blend the wool, polyester and viscose fibres in varying proportions.
    3 – The blended fibres are then carded to produce webs of parallel fibres.
  4 & 5 – The webs are layered together in alternating directions to form a thick batt.
    6 – The batt is fed into the hardening machine.
    7 – The felt is subjected to heat, humidity and pressure.
    8 – Cylinders in the fulling machine.
Right:
  9 & 10 – Fulling strengthens the felt.
    11 – Rolls of finished felt.
Between fulling and packaging, the felt can also be treated in various ways, depending on its intended use (see overleaf).

The fulling process gives the felt cohesion and makes it stronger. It is then dried on a rack or drier bed, its edges are trimmed, and depending on its intended use, it may undergo various finishing treatments to change its appearance or properties. It is generally steam-treated to prevent curling and further shrinkage. Then it may be coated, heat-treated, or brushed to give a soft surface texture; trimmed or shaved to remove visible fibres; dyed, printed or starched; covered with adhesive film; shaped, punched or cut; or applied to other materials, such as metal, wood, foam rubber or polyurethane. Finally it is quality-controlled and then rolled and packaged for sale or shipping.

Left: Felt before it is pressed.

Opposite: Piles of felt straight from the machine.

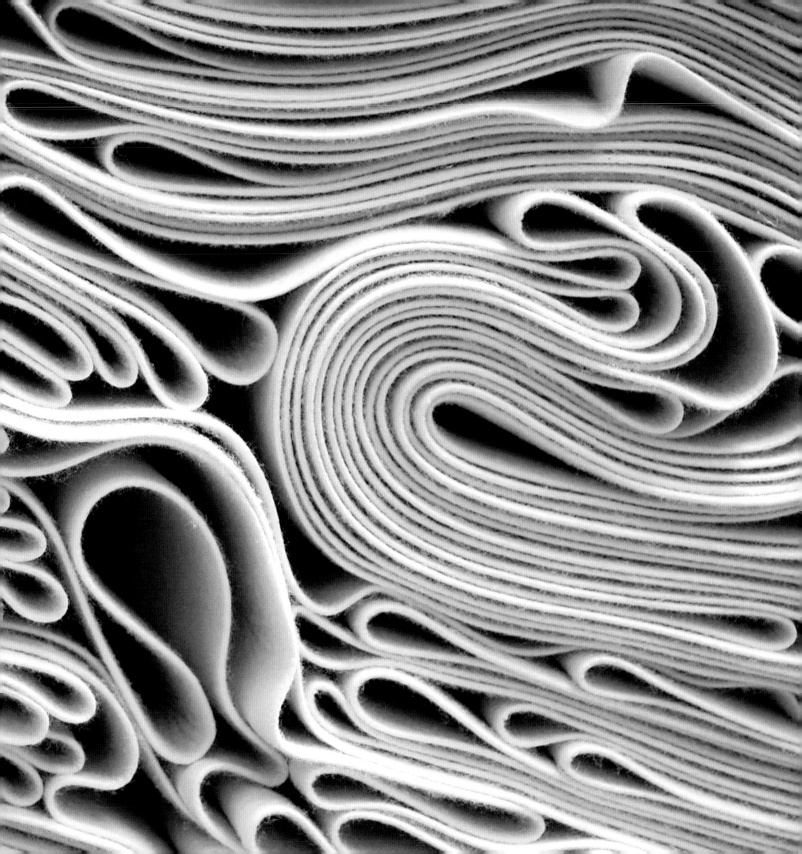

The dyeing process

Left:
Autoclaves in the dyeing room.
The process takes between 2 and 4 hours.
Right, from top to bottom:
Water is needed to dye the wool.
After dyeing, the felt is dried and its edges
are trimmed.

Stamping

Left, from top to bottom:
Stamping out felt bobs (used for polishing and cleaning).
The finished bobs.
A diagram on the wall shows cross-sections of a range of bobs, discs and buffs.

Right, from top to bottom:
Stamping self-adhesive felt discs.
Stamping felt seals for car engines.
The leftover sheets of felt.

Opposite: Felt discs sorted and packed, ready for delivery.

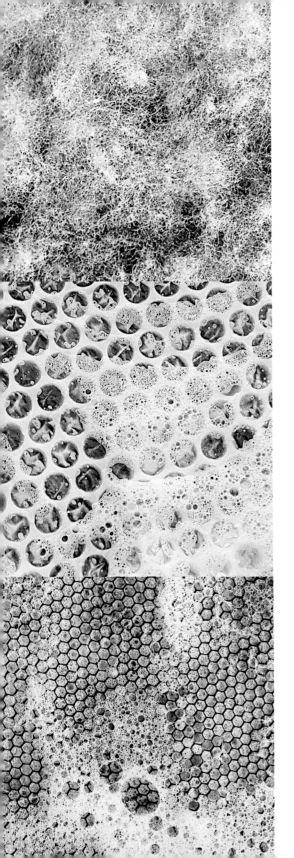

Wet felting by hand

The basic requirements for making felt at home are the same as those needed industrially: heat, moisture and friction. It's best to work out of doors or in the bathroom to avoid getting the carpet wet. If you're working on a polished floor, protect it with a plastic sheet or a wooden board.

• Use carded wool or untreated knitting yarn.

• Begin by laying out a fairly even layer of wool on a sheet of bubble wrap or plastic mesh. (I prefer to use a synthetic mesh with large holes, in order to keep a close feel on the material, but at the start it's important to lay the mesh on the wool and lift it up a few times, to check that it will not catch on the fibres.) Try to keep most of the threads running in the same direction, and avoid creating bulky spots or holes. Lay out another layer of wool on top of the first, changing the direction of the threads so the new layer is perpendicular to the first. Repeat the same process several times, alternating the direction each time.

• Now you can work on the decoration. Arrange larger areas of colour on the base layers first, followed by smaller details. Some practice will definitely be needed before you master this stage, because any subtle effects you try to create at this point will change radically during the felting process. The fabric will become denser and heavier, so that transparent or coloured layers may look attractive when first added but will change and turn opaque, and scattered fibres intended to create delicate patterns could risk turning into rough and lumpy splodges. At the beginning, therefore, it may often seem like the end result looks nothing like the intermediate stages, but the same uncertainty can also create pleasant surprises.

Previous pages:

Wet felting by hand

Left, from top to bottom:
Check the wool fibre for impurities, scrunch it up and using a sheet of bubble wrap as a base, build up a series of alternating layers.
Carefully place a piece of fine mesh fabric over the top and soak it with hot soapy water.
Lay the felt on a bamboo mat, then roll it up firmly and unroll it. Repeat until you are satisfied with the results.

Right: The finished piece of felt.

Opposite:
Accidental felting can occur inside a damp wardrobe. Almost everyone knows the feeling of pulling out a favourite jumper only to find that it has become thick, stiff and unwearable!

With experience, you can learn to recognize these happy accidents and recreate them in future projects.

• Cover it with a layer of fine mesh fabric and pour on hot soapy water, thoroughly soaking the wool fibres and squashing down the fluffy layers. Cover with another layer of bubble wrap and pour on a few drops of very hot soapy water. Rub very slowly over the top, carefully lifting up the bubble wrap occasionally and flipping it over. When the wet felt is relatively even and flat, roll it up inside a bamboo table mat or sushi mat. Roll and unroll several times, pressing down and increasing the pressure as you go. Finally, rinse the felt and let it dry naturally. It will shrink, so if the size is no longer large enough for your needs, you will need to start over. With practice, you will start to recognize when to stop.

• It is also possible to make felt in a washing machine. (It can also happen by accident, ruining a favourite sweater in the process by making it shrink and become bulky and hard.) Practice is needed to get good results from this type of wet felting. Place the fibres you want to felt between two pieces of fine mesh cloth. Then stitch the layers together, using large running stitches all over the surface. Set the washing machine to a short, cool program (35–40° C). When the wash has finished, take off the mesh and allow the felt to dry.

Felt is an excellent material for experimenting with, and this book only explores a selection of possible projects. More adventurous techniques could include making three-dimensional objects such as hats and slippers, capturing moving threads under a resin coating, and felting wool over a metallic base layer (see page 157).

Needle felting

Industrial needle felt

In this form of feltmaking, the entangling of the fibres is done mechanically. Because of this, the raw materials used do not need to be of animal origin; they may be of plant origin, synthetic or a combination. This means that costs are much lower. These non-wovens are used in the fields of industry, horticulture, home decoration (e.g. wall and floor coverings), car production, health and hygiene.

This type of felting is done with special needles that have barbed ends. They are fixed in long rows (2 or 3 metres) inside the machines, at a density of anything from 50 to 300 needles per centimetre. These punch through the webs of carded fibres and gradually tangle them together. Some machines have two layers of needles, one above and one below the fabric.

Wet felting in a washing machine

Opposite, from top to bottom:
First create a layer of wool fibre or yarn.
Sandwich it between two layers of fine mesh fabric and stitch the whole thing together loosely.
Place in a cool wash cycle (35–40° C, depending on the yarn being used).
After washing, unpick the protective layers of linen and let the felt dry.

Right:
Craft felt is available in a wide range of colours.

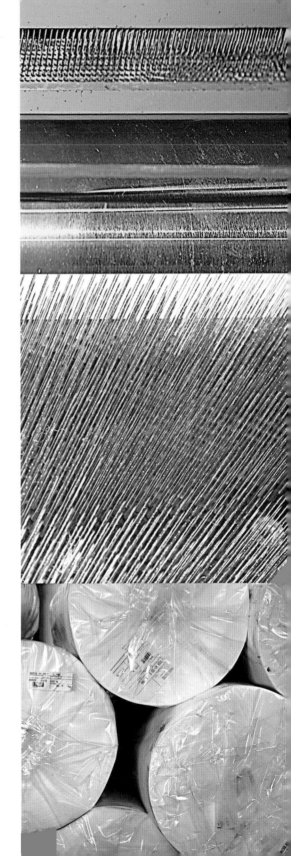

Industrial needle felting at
the Sedan factory, France

Opposite:
The basic fibres in their raw state.

Left, from top to bottom:
The raw fibres in storage.
These are thoroughly mixed together in
varying proportions in humid conditions.

Right, from top to bottom:
Front view of a needle felting machine.
A needle plate.
The finished rolls of felt, packaged and ready
for shipping.

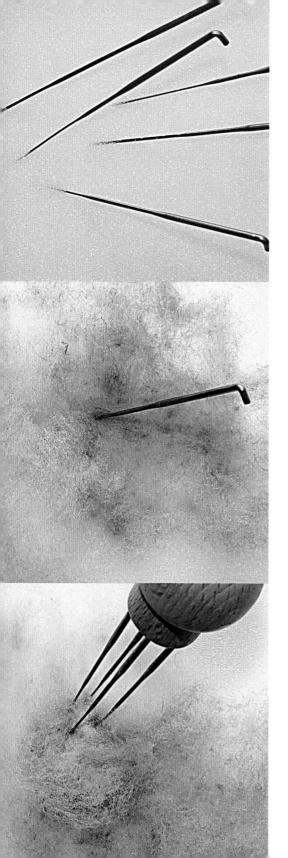

Needle felting by hand

Needle felting is now becoming an increasingly popular handicraft, particularly for projects such as toys and jewelry. Felting needles, protective polyurethane foam and carded wool fibre in a huge range of colours are all available from specialist craft shops, department stores and online suppliers. You can also dye your own fibre or re-dye commercially dyed wool – magenta, sky blue or lemon yellow – to achieve a multitude of subtle shades.

Felting needles come in different sizes and should be selected according to the effect you want to achieve. Very fine needles are good for detailed work, and create only small holes that are easily disguised, but they can also break rather easily and are quite expensive.

Needle felting is done by placing wool or other fibres on top of a protective foam base, and pushing the needle through fibres again and again, tangling and fixing them together. It's important to be very careful and avoid accidentally stabbing yourself with the sharp needle. The needle should be firmly pushed in, moving in a straight up-and-down motion, and it's wise to wear protective glasses in case a needle suddenly breaks. If you are felting a large surface area, you can use a felting tool that holds four, six or more needles, which will help you to make faster progress.

Needle felting by hand

Left, from top to bottom:
Different weights of needle on top of the protective foam backing. Needle felting the wool on a foam base. Make sure that you thrust the needle firmly through in a straight motion, to avoid breaking it. For larger pieces, a felting tool with multiple needles can be used.

If you're very keen to pursue large-scale projects, it's possible to buy a home needle felting machine. Several brands are available; they are a similar size and shape to a sewing machine, and have a needle foot that holds 5 or 7 needles.

For craft professionals, a larger, bulkier machine is also available, with changeable feet incorporating between 7 and 76 needles. The speed of work attainable with this type of machine is incredible, as are the results.

Needle felting machines allow you to felt with materials other than wool, including a wide range of synthetics and mixed fibres. The finished felts can also be reversible. One side is soft, fluffy felt, and the other side may either be the same, or may be studded with small needle holes (sometimes these are almost invisible, depending on the fibres used). The fibres merge together and form patterns and motifs, which can either be solid or with open spaces, creating a new piece of fabric as if by magic.

Needle felting with a home felting machine

Right, from top to bottom:
The needle foot at work. If you want to create a freestanding piece of felt, it's best to use a soluble non-woven as a base fabric, scattering the fibres on top of it.
On one side of the fabric, the needle holes are visible.
On the other side, the fabric looks soft and fluffy. Wash the felt to dissolve the non-woven support and let your finished felt dry.

Industrial tufting

Left:
The machine is fed by a huge number of reels of thread.

Right, above:
The tufting needles at work. The threads are fed in at the top and the reverse of the fabric can be seen below.

Right, below:
In the foreground on the left, the right side of the fabric and its non-woven support.

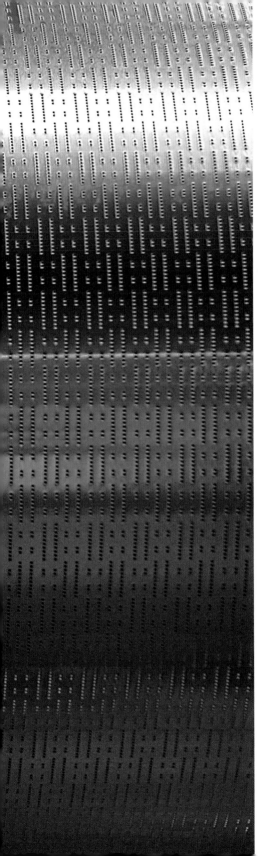

Finishing

Opposite:
A cylinder.

Right, from top to bottom:
Applying glue to the reverse side.
A test printing on a square of fabric.
Printing.

Tufting

Industrial tufting

This technique is used to create rugs and carpets, and can sometimes resemble needle felting. Similar hooked needles are used, but they are positioned on the reverse of the support fabric: a strong non-woven. As they pass through the fabric, they carry a yarn which, on the right side, is pulled up by to form a loop (creating a spongy pile) or a loop which is then sheared (forming a velvety pile). The tufts of yarn are packed closely together in rows across the length of the fabric. For this reason, the finished product may be relatively fragile; if one loop is pulled, the whole row will unravel. To prevent this, a protective coating is generally applied to the reverse.

Industrial tufting

A close-up view of some tufted carpets.
A strengthening layer is added on the reverse side.

From top to bottom:
Chiné tufted pile.
Printed tufted pile.
Trimmed and printed tufted pile.

Hand tufting

Like needle felting, tufting is used to create handcrafted rugs. The tufts of yarn are passed through the support fabric using a pneumatic tufting gun.

By hand, tufting can be done using the same kind of hooked needle that is used for needle felting, on a range of backing fabrics including canvas and mesh. A loop of yarn on one side of the support becomes a tuft on the other. An adhesive non-woven can be ironed on to the reverse side of the fabric to strengthen it and prevent unravelling.

A similar effect can be achieved through Cornely embroidery. The Cornely sewing machine uses a hook instead of a needle to create looped chain stitches, which can be built up into a dense textured pattern. Tambour embroidery is a hand-embroidery method that uses a similar hook to form dense chains of stitches. There are also various knitting, crochet and weaving techniques that also create looped or spongy fabrics.

Hand tufting

From top to bottom:
On top of a protective foam base, a hooked needle is used
to push yarn through a mesh backing from the reverse side.
The loops of yarn on the right side.
The same pile, brushed for effect.

Felt designs:
the sky's the limit!

Sunlight through the clouds

(Stratus nebulosus)

If you have never tried making felt by hand, it
may well seem like a dull and fiddly activity, but
you'll soon come to see that this isn't the case
when you first get a feel for the fabric changing
shape in your hands. For my first-ever attempts
at feltmaking, I used a washing machine, thinking
that this would make the process much quicker
and easier, but the results were disappointing.
During a rough felting process of this kind, the
fabric shrinks down and becomes very tough
and hard. The surface becomes wrinkled and
puckered, and it's impossible to undo the felting
and go back to the previous stage. When this
happens industrially, the felt can be brushed and
smoothed, but at home it's much harder to
salvage. If you really do want to find a use for it,
the best thing to do, surprisingly, is to try to break
it down and tear it into pieces. The following
pages along with pages 65 and 66 will give you
some ideas.

Previous pages: Fields shrouded in mist.

Felt lace and fleecy effects
(Altocumulus stratiformis translucidus perlucidus)

Here's an idea for using pieces of felt that have come out crinkled and tough. Using a lot of elbow grease and the right kind of sturdy tools (such as a vice and some pliers), it may be possible to tear the felt into small pieces, which can then be shaped with a craft knife (be careful not to hurt yourself). Here, the pieces have been pinned onto a sheet of soluble plastic and then joined together with freely worked machine embroidery, created using an embroidery foot. The textile is then washed so that the soluble support dissolves away. This type of fabric would team up well with woollen fleece to decorate a range of clothes and accessories.

A cloudless sky

The sky is never a single colour; even when it seems clear, you can always see graduations in shade, from grey to white, from pale blue to bright blue, or from blue to orange, via yellow and deep ochre.

To create felt in graduating shades, begin as you would for a single-colour piece, by building up several layers of wool fibre which will form the base (see page 22). Then to create the decoration, tear wool fibres in various shades into fine pieces and carefully scatter them over the base. Cover with linen or mesh, pour on hot soapy water and then press very carefully so that the top layer of fibres stays in position. Once the wool is thoroughly soaked, press it down and continue the felting process.

This technique creates interesting and subtle effects that look good used in combination with solid colours or more complex motifs.

Cirrus floccus (overleaf)

A bright blue sky is brought to life by jaunty little
clouds that almost resemble puffs of smoke from a
pipe. Small pieces of wool fibre are scattered in a lively
way across a ground of cotton print in graduating
shades of blue, then needle felted by hand. Try
creating similar patterns in different colourways.

Cirrus floccus
See previous pages.

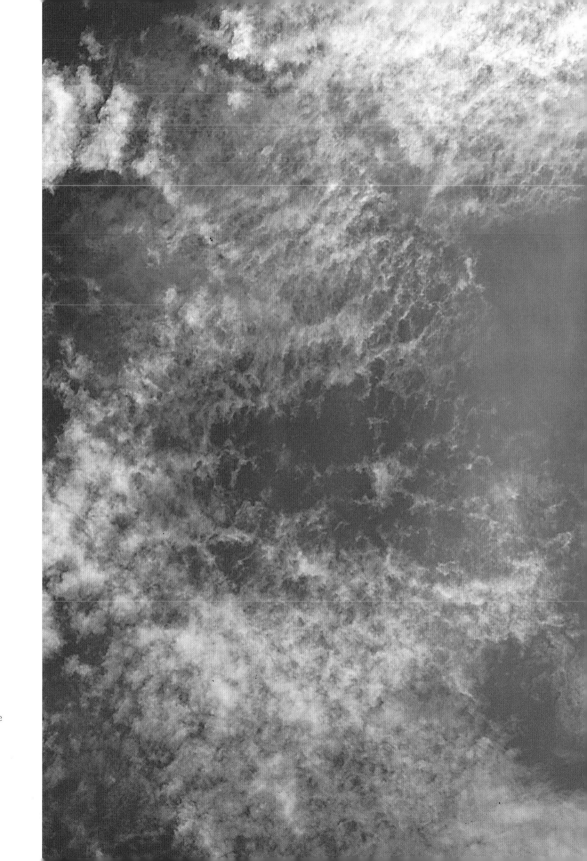

Opposite:
The dancing clouds in the foreground are cirrus humilis and fractus. Along the horizon, the little clouds in rows are cumulus humilis radiatus, while high in the sky are cirrus spissatus.

Right:
Cirrocumulus lacunosus.

Fine strands of cloud
(Cirrus fibratus vertebratus)

These wispy clouds stream out from a central
point, as supple and fluid as flowing locks of hair.
If you want to make your own version of these
clouds, acrylic fibres work better than wool,
which is thicker and gives a more matte effect.
The fabric opposite was created by needle felting
on a machine, on a ground of soft wool.

Overleaf: A bank of cirrus fibratus clouds.

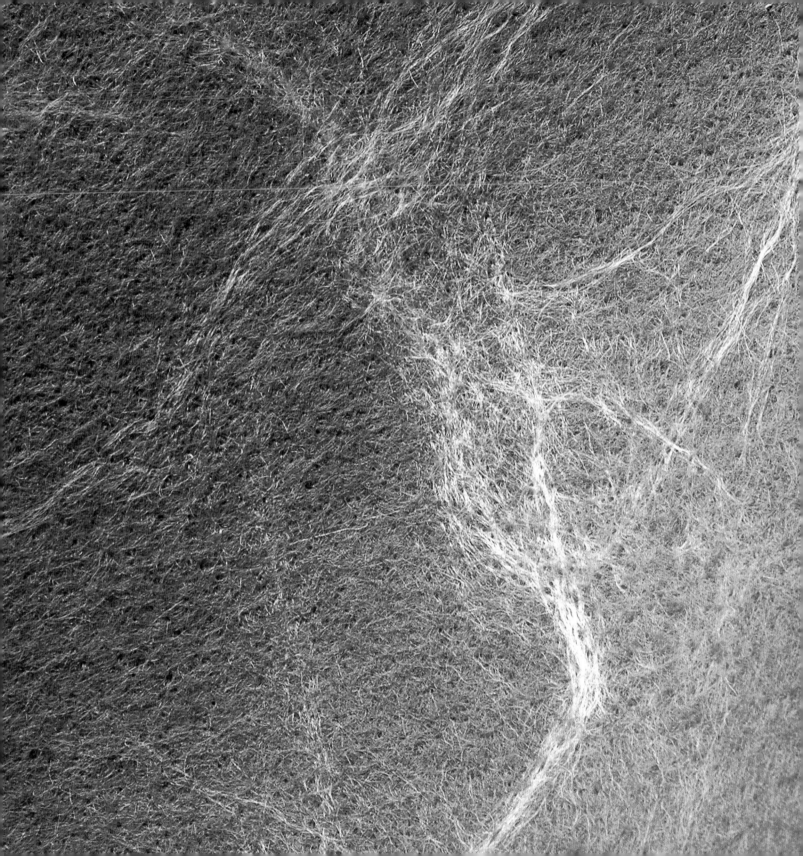

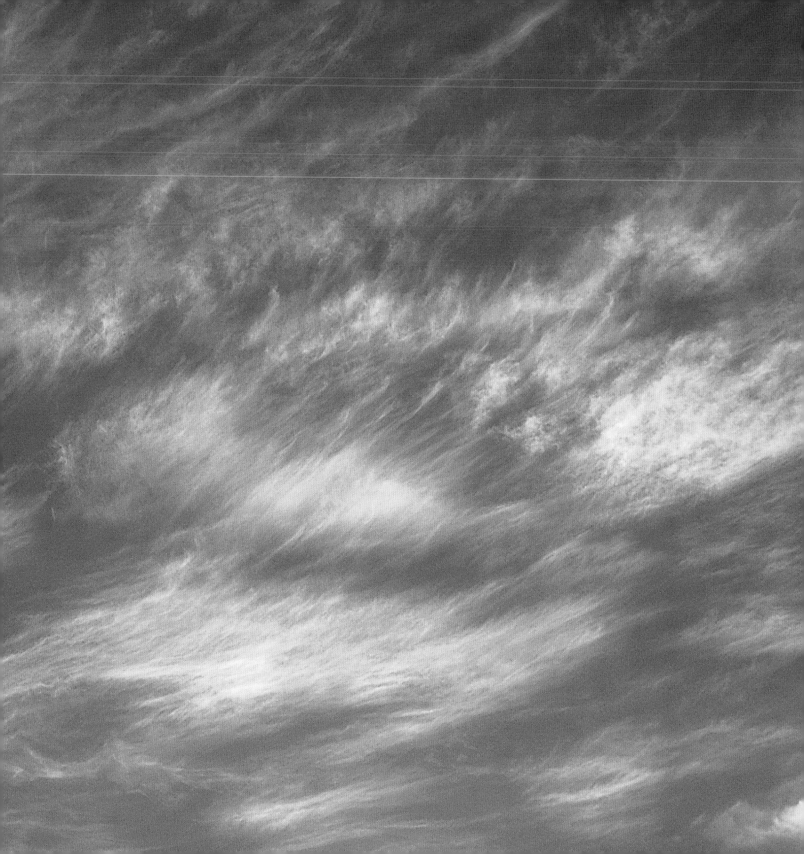

Cirrus in flight

The image on the right makes use of the tufting technique. Begin with a flannel base, and embroider some lines in back stitch with a sewing machine. Then, on the reverse, position a 'cloud' of wool fibre in a similar shade to the embroidery or the background, and use a tufting needle to fix it in place, forming soft, blurry shapes like those found in pastel sketches. If the tufted areas become too dense, you can use tweezers to thin out the fibres.

Cirrus spissatus (overleaf)

I'm not alone in loving clouds of this type. They are so soft and light, so elegant, and can take on the most wonderful range of shapes. Sailing calmly and seductively through the sky at a height between 6,000 and 12,500 metres (19,500 and 40,000 ft), they are the most distant of clouds. They are made up of ice crystals, scattered and blown by strong winds, and this is what gives them their silky texture and striking shapes.

This is another tufted fabric. Pull apart clumps of wool fibre in various colours and scatter them over a base. Needle felt all over, then turn the fabric over and comb it with a firm brush, and finally iron it. To strengthen the fabric, you could apply an iron-on adhesive backing to the reverse.

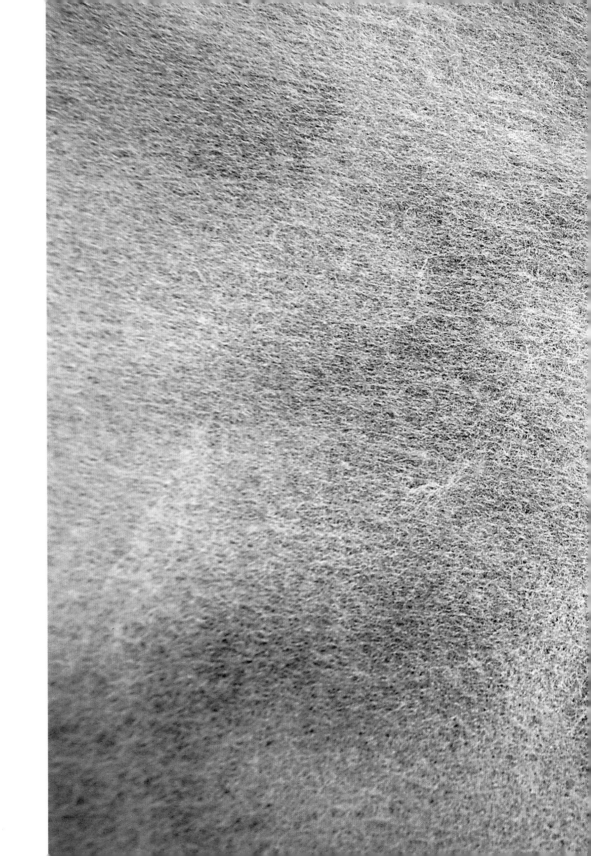

Cirrus spissatus clouds (**opposite**)
and turned into a tufted textile (**right**).

A flock of sheep
(Altocumulus stratiformis)

Low clouds are made up of a host of water droplets hanging in the air. They scatter the sunlight in all directions, diffusing and softening it. To begin this piece, wool fibre in a range of matching tones is needle felted over a base of polystyrene foam, to create a delicately coloured layer of fragile and transparent felt. The cloud shapes are then cut from this layer and fixed to the ground fabric with needle felting.

Cotton wool sky (overleaf)
(Cirrocumulus floccus)

Form little balls of wool by hand, using a felting needle. Then use needle felting to fix them to a ground of coloured lace. Finish with a sewing machine with a needle felting foot.

Cotton wool sky

(see previous pages)

Silky flakes

(see overleaf)

Silky flakes
(Altocumulus floccus)

Use a piece of cotton fabric as a background. Tear up some small pieces of felt (see page 44) and scatter them over the base, then needle felt them by hand, leaving the edges of the clouds deliberately loose. You could also fix them down with embroidery stitches. Keep working across the background until it is filled with clouds (as shown opposite).

Right:
Cirrus spissatus clouds form amazing smooth white shapes when blown by the wind.

Dappled skies

The effect shown opposite requires a base fabric of wool, knit or felt, or you could make your own with needle felting. To do this, begin by carding a fine transparent web with parallel fibres. Then make another and place it over the top, with the fibres running perpendicular to the first layer. Add a third layer in the same way, and another if needed. Then loosely needle felt the layers together, using a multi-needle felting tool.

To create the three-dimensional shapes, needle felt some small balls of fibre and attach them to the background, still using the felting tool. Arrange them in a random fashion, with variations in size and density. Then felt the whole fabric gently in the washing machine to make it stronger.

This technique could be turned into a warm jumper or jacket, or a cosy bedspread.

Overleaf:
A panoramic view of dappled clouds.

More dappled skies

This jacquard knit is done by hand with yarn dyed in different colours; the bobbles are a different shade from the background. The ground is a basic rib (first row: 1 knit, 1 purl, and repeat to the end of the row; second row: 1 purl, 1 knit, etc.). The bobbles (knit 5 stitches into 1 stitch, 3 rows of stocking stitch then knit the 5 stitches together) are freely arranged; sometimes isolated, sometimes forming bands or clusters. In the densest areas, they occur every 4 stitches. To avoid creating floating threads on the reverse, the yarn for the bobbles is knitted into the knit stitches on the right side and into the purl stitches on the reverse.

When the knit is finished, felt it lightly, or wait until it has been washed and then felt it.

This effect is great for cosy clothes for children or for home accessories, but it is best to restrict it to fairly small items if you want quick results.

Strings of pearls

(see overleaf)

Strings of pearls
(Altocumulus perlucidus)

1 – Choose a base fabric, such as a fleecy knit, and stretch it out over an embroidery frame.
2 – Make small balls from needle felted wool and fix them to the background with a few stitches.
3 – Use couching to cover the balls in fancy thread, building up a pattern of curves and swirls across the rest of the ground in the same way.

These clouds have a dainty, feminine feel. They would look good on throw cushions or perhaps decorating a hat.

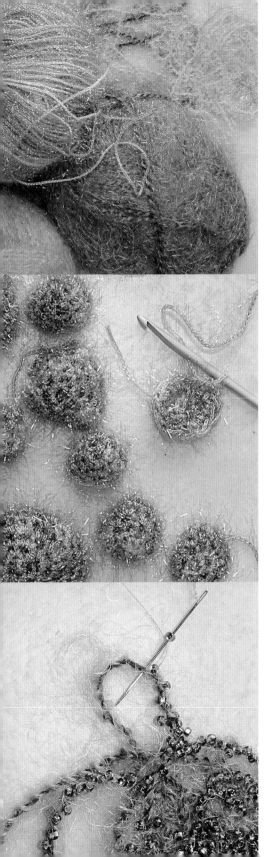

Icy droplets

1 – The base is made by needle felting (see page 31) using fancy yarn in shades of grey.

2 – The bobbles are crocheted, using yarn with a sparkling, frosty look. Chain 3 stitches; stitch through the first stitch in the chain, closing the ring; chain 1. Then stitch twice through each stitch in the circle to make it bigger, to a diameter of 1 to 2 cm (½ to 1 in.), then once through each stitch to add height (for one or two rows), then stop. Vary the size of each bobble by altering the number of stitches and rows. Stitch these shapes discreetly to the base.

3 – Stitch on iridescent or translucent grey beads, accentuating the effect of light and shade.

This technique could be used for fashion or home accessories, and would also work well as an individual motif on a jacket or skirt, for example.

Giant fluffy tufts

This technique is not true tufting but an adapted version designed to achieve a similar effect on a much larger scale.

1 – Take a piece of felt, 3 to 5 mm (⅛ to ¼ in.) thick, and using a large hole-punch, make a scattered pattern of holes, approximately 10 mm (½ in.) across.

2 – Next, make woollen balls of different sizes, ranging between 15 and 30 mm (¾ and 1 ½ in.), by needle felting over a foam base. Leave a piece of wool sticking out on one side as a 'handle'. Then glue around this point, close to the ball of felt, and thread it through one of the holes in the base fabric. Press it down, let it dry, and trim off any excess.

3 – Repeat across the whole surface, creating variations in size and density.

The same balls of needle felted wool could also be sewn onto a fleecy fabric for a soft and cosy effect.

Overleaf:
Fluffy white cumulus congestus clouds.

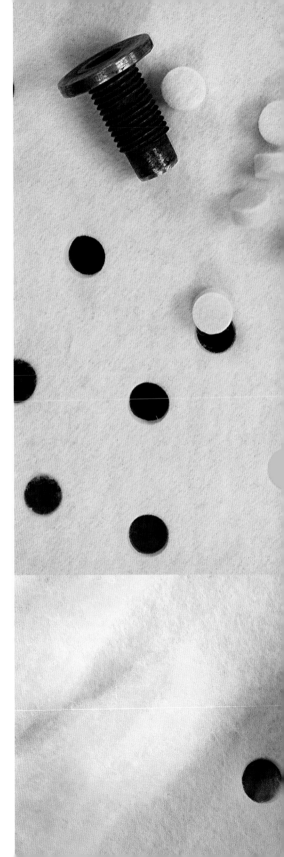

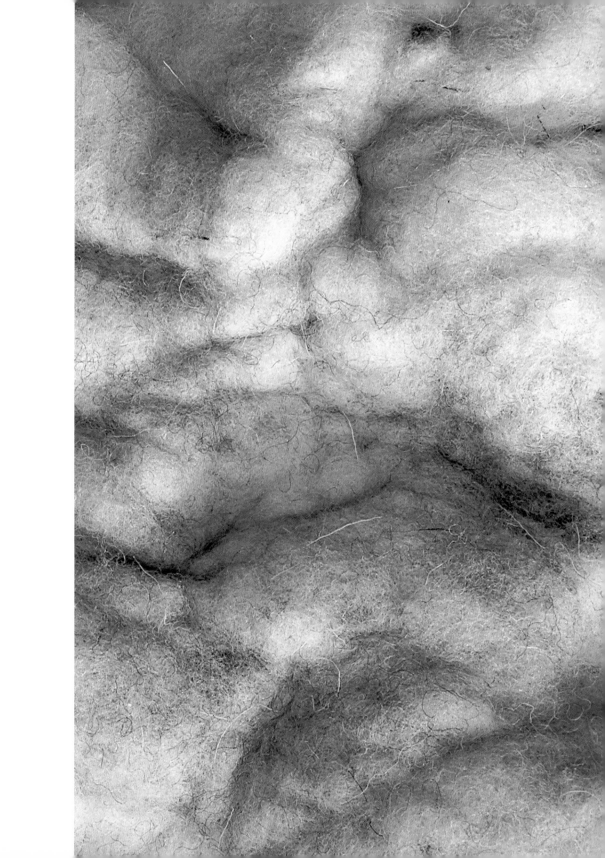

A blanket of clouds
(Cumulus and altocumulus)

The textile opposite was created on a base of flexible stainless steel mesh, which was covered on both sides with grey and cream wool fibre. The whole piece is needle felted in places and then wet felted by hand (see page 22).

The finished piece has a 'memory' and can be curved and uncurved into different shapes. It could be used for warming up stiff necks, bad backs and minor twists and sprains.

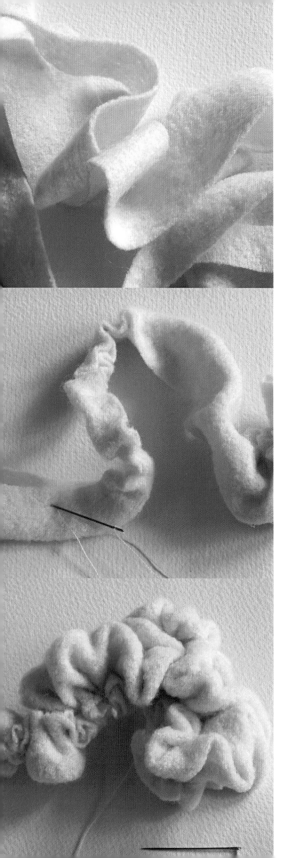

Fleecy twists

Here's a three-dimensional lace effect created with wool fabric.

1 – Cut out strips of boiled wool in varying widths, from 2.5 to 7.5 cm (1 to 3 in.).

2 – Fold each strip in half and with a strong thread, use running stitch to join the two edges together.

3 – Pull on the thread to gather up the strip, forming irregular curves, and fix them with stitches to hold the shapes.

4 – Repeat for the rest of the strips, then join them together, creating a pattern of curves with lacy holes.

This textile could be used for an unusual jacket, a bedspread or a soft rug.

Cloudy rug and cushion covers (overleaf)

Industrial felt offcuts (see page 20) have been used to make an oversized rug. Smaller pieces could make matching cushion covers or a throw.

This technique is generally used for embroidery projects, at a much smaller scale. Changing scales does not always work but it is often an interesting exercise. It involves making adaptations, using unusual materials, and discovering new ways of working, but it can lead to very exciting results.

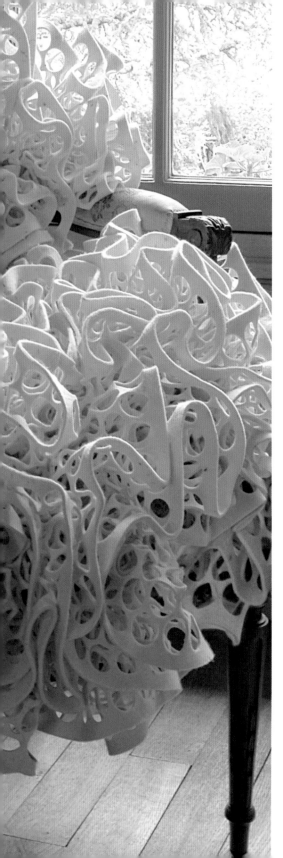

The basic materials for this rug were offcuts from the Mouzon felt factory, but similar offcuts are sometimes available from craft suppliers. Punching all these holes in felt fabric by hand is theoretically possible but very time-consuming!

This pierced strip of felt is 15 cm (6 in.) wide and 7 mm (¼ in.) thick. For simplicity and for aesthetic reasons, a base material has not been used. The method used is similar to the 'Fleecy twists' on page 86. Thread a very strong cotton yarn through the row of holes 5 cm (2 in.) from one of the edges of the strip, rather than through the centre row of holes; this will give the finished piece a denser look on one side and a looser, more dynamic look on the other. Pull this thread and gather the strip to form a frill. Arrange the gathered strip in a series of curves, twisting it every 20 cm (8 in.) or so to meet the previous loop, alternating the directions and fixing the twists in position with stitches where required. This will create a series of meandering loops, forming a lively surface that can be expanded to any size required.

Previous pages:
The denser side of the looped mat.

Left and opposite:
The looser side has more holes and space.

Droplets of light

Felt discs are used in industry for a wide range of
purposes, such as polishing, filtration and as shock-
absorbers. But with a little inspiration they can also be
used creatively to make unusual home accessories
such as lampshades, napkin rings and throws.

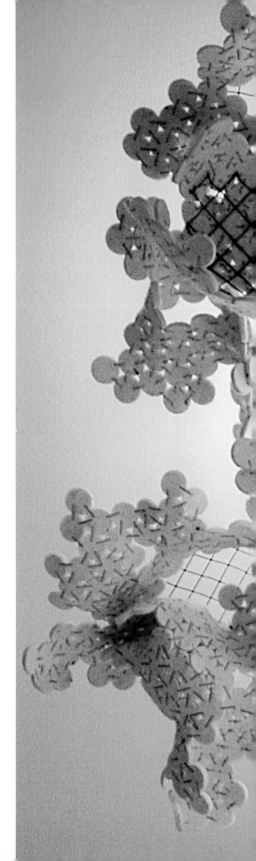

1 – The lampshade is made by joining 1 cm (½ in.) felt discs together with staples. Begin by making small clusters of discs and then join those clusters together to make loose shapes. Use a hammer to flatten the staples. Next, cut some wire mesh into pieces of varied sizes and shapes. Bend and shape this as desired, and fix it in position with staples. Work very carefully and wear protective gloves.

2 & 3 – Use staples to fix the felt pieces to the wire framework, adding some extra scattered felt discs as desired.

4 & 5 – Fit the whole piece around an old lampshade frame. Close it with temporary clips and check that it looks good from all angles. Make any adjustments necessary and join the edges together permanently with fine wire. You may need help installing it on a working light fitting. It's important to choose a low-wattage bulb. The finished shade will create a delicate pattern of shadows.

6 – The napkin ring is made from the same stapled felt discs as the lampshade. You could also use embroidery stitches to fix the discs together.

Textured towers

Here, felt discs in varying numbers (anywhere from 2 to 15) are threaded onto strong thread like beads on a string. The thread goes through the top disc and back down through the pile, where it is finished off firmly. The resulting 'towers' of felt are then arranged on a base fabric to form patterns of different heights, and then stitched or glued down.

This would make an unusual throw, with the undulating pattern of the felt towers giving a real sense of movement.

A cloud to sleep under (overleaf)

Use a strong thread in a shade that matches the woollen base. String the felt discs onto the thread like beads, but this time, work in all directions to create a surface with volume and a variety of dense and open spaces. Cut the edges of the base fabric to form an irregular, cloud-like shape. Fix the felt garlands firmly but discreetly to the base, covering it all the way up to the edges.

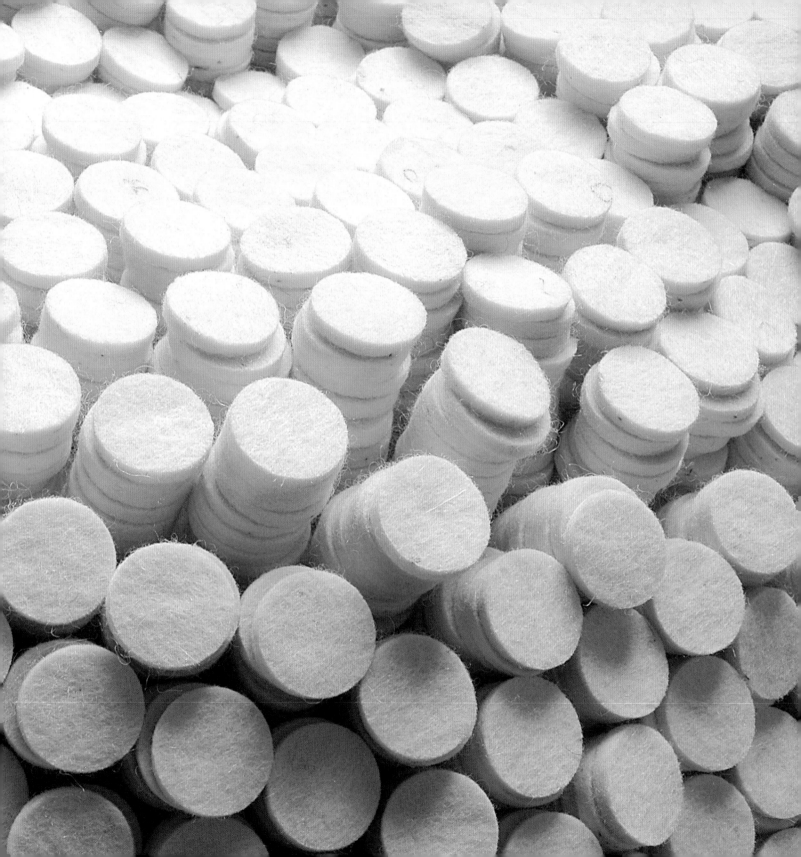

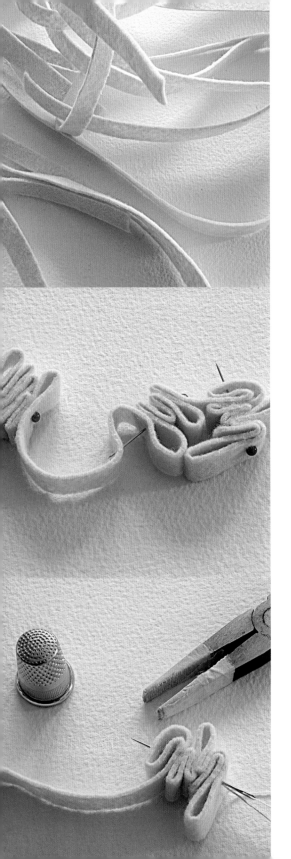

Flattening the sky

(see overleaf)

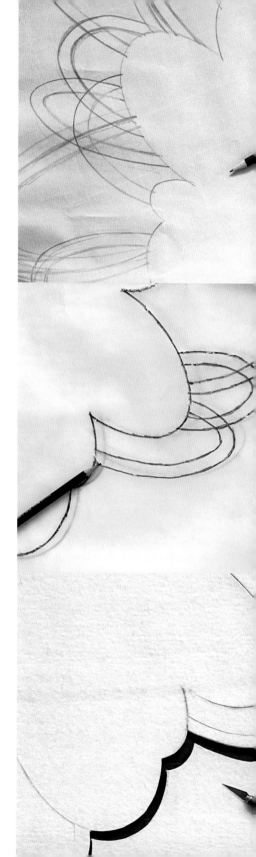

Flattening the sky (previous pages)

Making use of the edges of felt fabric can be fun, but the neat curves and flat lines are not very cloud-like. However, this flatness can be put to good use in this striking table mat.

1 – Cut out bands of felt, 1 cm (½ in.) wide.

2 – Curl each band into an irregular series of meandering curves and fix them with pins.

3 – Stitch through with strong thread, using a thimble and some pliers with taped ends to protect your fingers and the needle.

4 – Take the stitched pieces and arrange them however you like. Pin in place and stitch together (concealing the thread in the felt pile) or glue.

The shadow of a cloud

This mat is made from felt with a thickness of 6 mm (¼ in.) or more.

1 – Begin by sketching a lifesize design on card, keeping your arm loose to create pleasing curves. Then copy it onto tracing paper. You could also start with a small-scale design and enlarge it using the grid method.

2 – Place the tracing paper pattern over the felt.

3 – Cut out the pattern with a craft knife, using a cutting board underneath and making sure that the knife follows the curves of your design.

You could choose to leave this mat plain and simple, or you could add interest by punching a scattered pattern of punched holes (left) or by sticking on some curved cut-out pieces to give a sense of depth and complexity (opposite).

Overleaf:
The intricately twisting edges of clouds resemble fractals, a series of fragmented geometric shapes made up of small parts that echo the form of the whole.

Little grey clouds, all in a row
(Cumulus humilis, with altocumulus above)

To create these little clouds, I've used a two-colour marl. Wind the yarn around two or three fingers on one hand, between 5 and 10 times. Take off the ring of yarn, place it under greaseproof paper and iron it. Then place it between two sheets of soluble non-woven and felt with a needle felting machine. Take off the top layer of non-woven and continue needle felting. Wash to dissolve the non-woven base and leave to dry.

Use needle felting or a few stitches to fix the clouds to a background of speckled fleece. This border motif would make an attractive edging for a fleece jacket.

The sky grows darker (overleaf)

As they grow larger, cumulus humilis clouds become cumulus mediocris, then cumulus congestus, and finally, perhaps cumulonimbus.

These larger clouds are made in the same way as those described above. They could be used as a motif on a blanket or knit, or needle felted together.

Opposite:
Grey clouds in two-colour marl
(see previous pages).

Overleaf:
Long rows of cumulus mediocris radiatus,
with a layer of cirrus spissatus above.

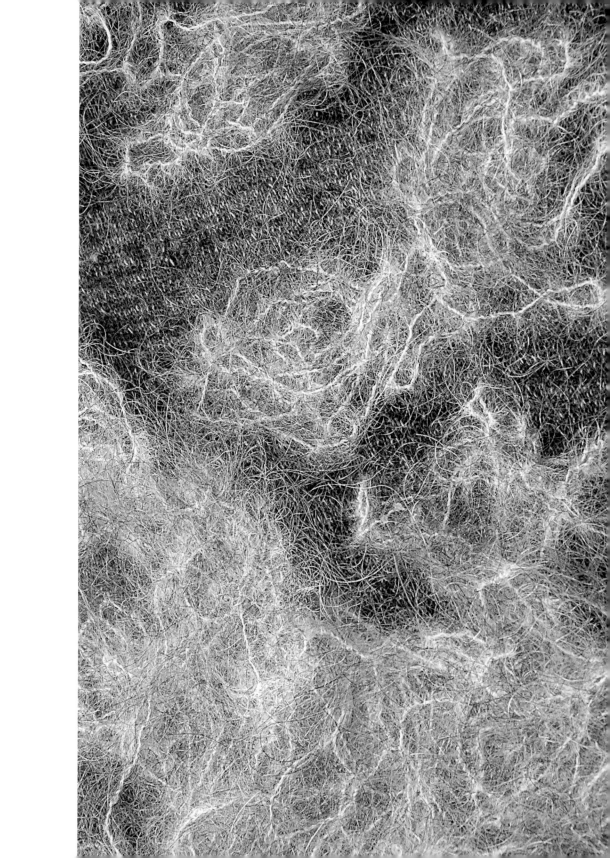

Wisps in the wind
(Cumulus fractus)

Each of these little grey clouds of mohair yarn is created by machine needle felting on a soluble non-woven base (see pages 30–31). They are arranged on a ground of denim-effect chiné knit in an irregular pattern, and fixed down with a single stitch. This makes the whole piece very light and allows the clouds to move in the breeze.

Swirling skies (overleaf)
(Cirrus fibratus and spissatus above banks of cirrocumulus)

For these clouds, wind the yarn several times around four fingers to form loose rings. Iron these flat and place them all between two layers of soluble non-woven. To give the final piece the feel of thick cloud, make sure that the small rings overlap each other. Pin the layers together and tack them, preferably with soluble thread. Needle felt by machine and then wash to dissolve the non-woven layers. Leave to dry.

You could also make the textile more solid by filling some of the flimsier areas with new rings of wool and needle felting again. This lacy fabric would make a striking scarf or camisole.

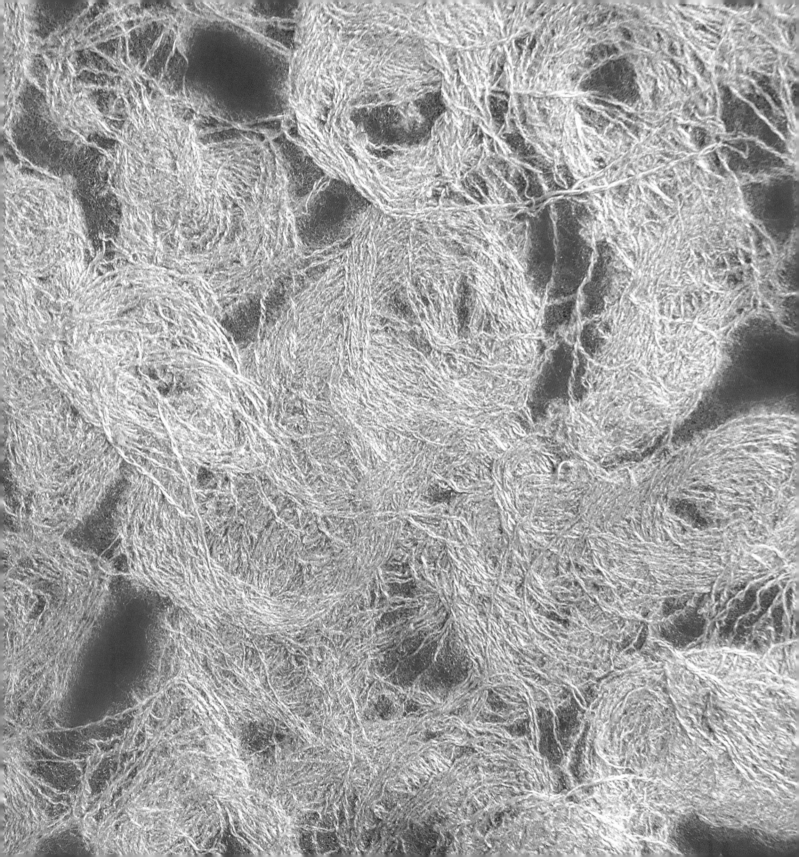

Swirling skies
(see previous pages)

Cloud banks are building
(Cumulus and stratocumulus with altocumulus)

This textile is made in the same way as the one
on the previous pages, but this time the needle
felting is done on alternate sides, creating a
contrast between flatter, denser areas and softer,
fluffier areas. It is also thicker than the previous
design. It would look good as a waistcoat or top.

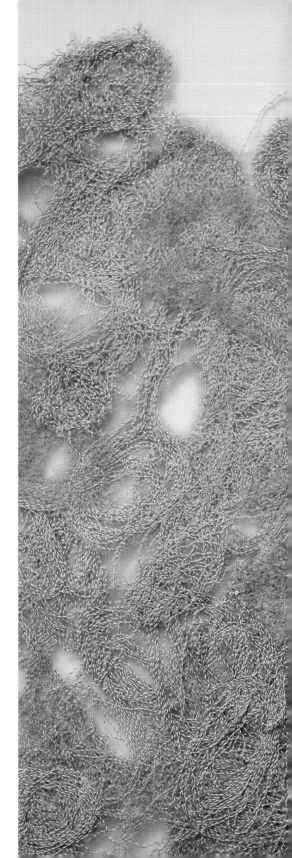

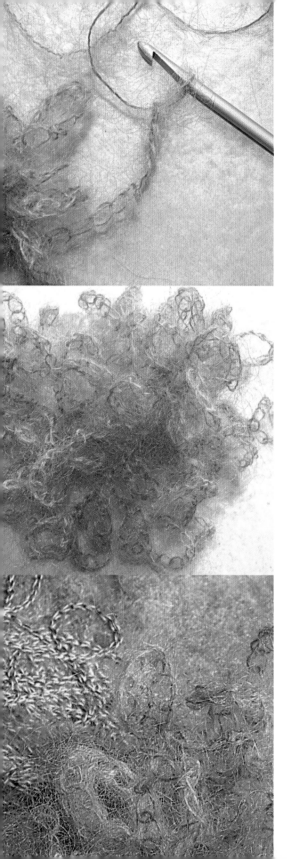

Grey fluffy swirls

1 – Using a fine mohair yarn and a medium crochet hook, *chain 12 stitches then stitch once into the first stitch (or third stitch, to make smaller circles) to close the loop,* then repeat several times from * to *.
To build up the volume of the cloud, stitch in between the first and second loops and start the process again, ending by stitching between another two of the loops, as desired.
2 – Continue to repeat the same steps to build up a voluminous cloud with loops on all sides.
3 – These clouds could be joined together to make a scarf or decorate a hat. They could also be used in combination with some of the flatter motifs shown on previous pages.

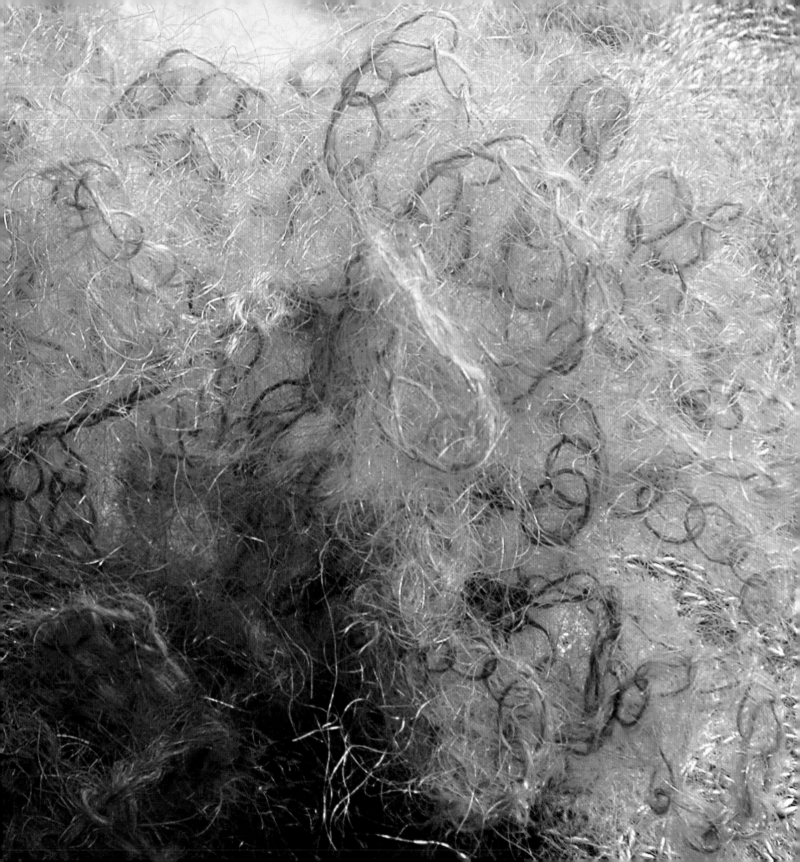

Crinkles of silk

If you layer wool fibre over silk fabric and wet felt it
(preferably by hand, to begin with), the piece will
look the same all over to begin with. However,
increased heat and friction will make the fibres move
across the surface, causing the silk to contract and
form attractive crinkles.

Try the technique with any kind of woven or
knitted silk, and then experiment with using
openwork fabrics.

Right side and reverse.

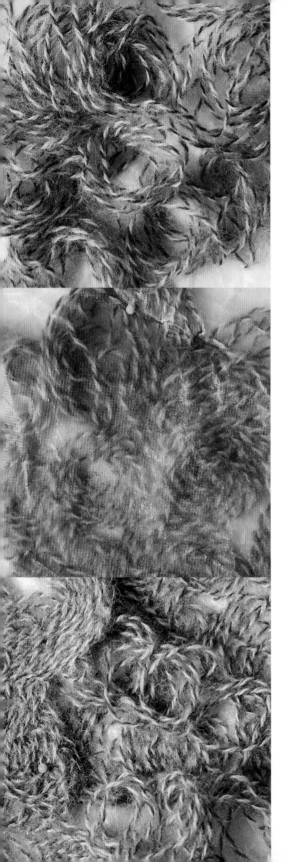

Weatherworn

This technique begins in the same way as those on pages 110 and 116.

1 – Build up a layer from swirls of yarn and iron it flat under greaseproof paper.

2 – Sandwich it between layers of soluble plastic or non-woven and begin needle felting, preferably by machine.

3 – Take off the top layer of non-woven and continue to needle felt. Then wash and leave to dry.

(overleaf)

Using elastic thread, making wide gathering stitches all over the textile. Gather and arrange as desired, creating a range of puckered and flat areas.

Holes in the sky (pages 128–129)
(Stratocumulus)

A similar technique, but this time worked in a very irregular way. By using fine synthetic yarns, you can create a cashmere-soft effect. A scarf or shawl in this method would make an original gift idea.

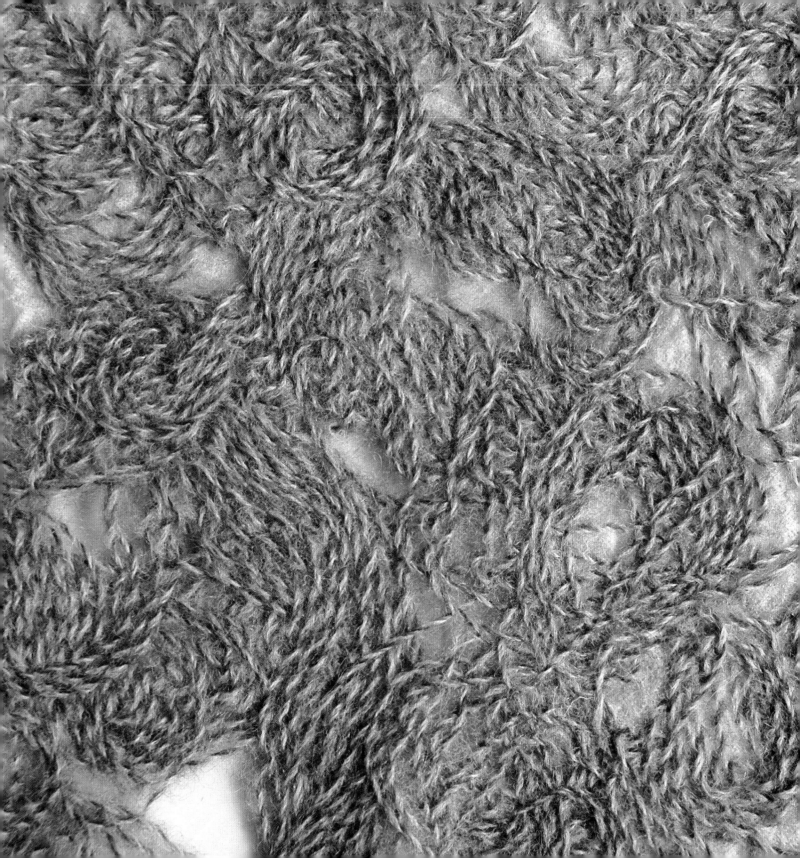

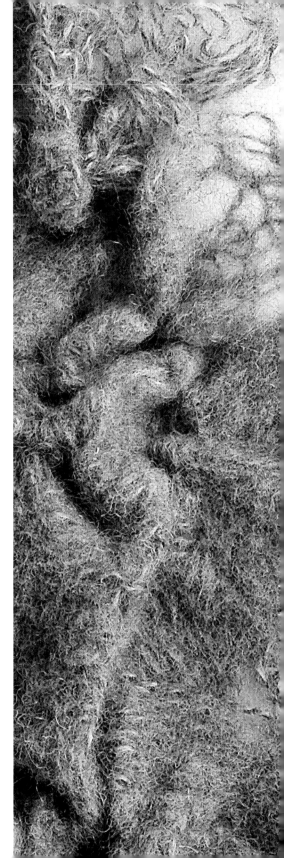

Weatherworn

Right side and reverse. Either side could be used, depending on the effect you want, to make a sexy mini-dress or a cosy bedjacket.

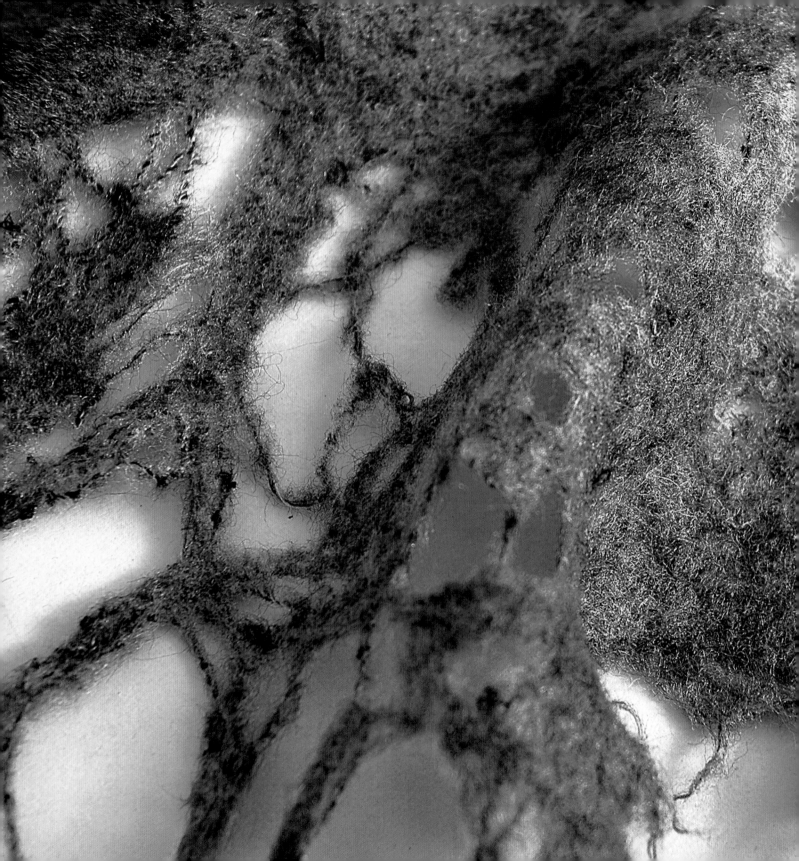

Opposite:
Holes in the sky (see previous pages)

Overleaf:
An overcast sky, with cumulus and
cumulonimbus praecipitatio clouds.

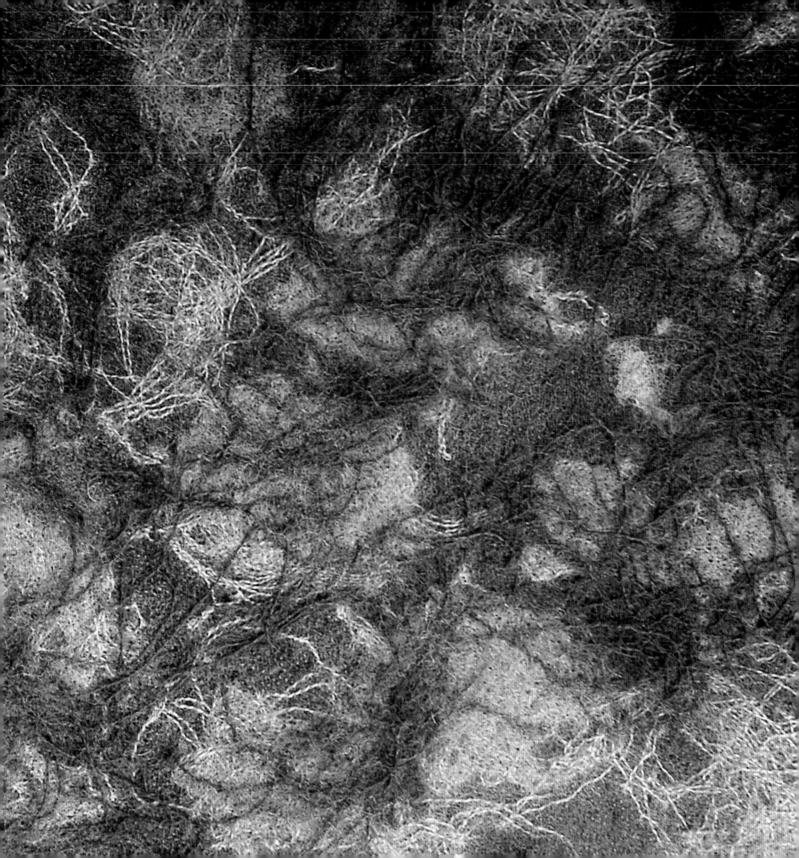

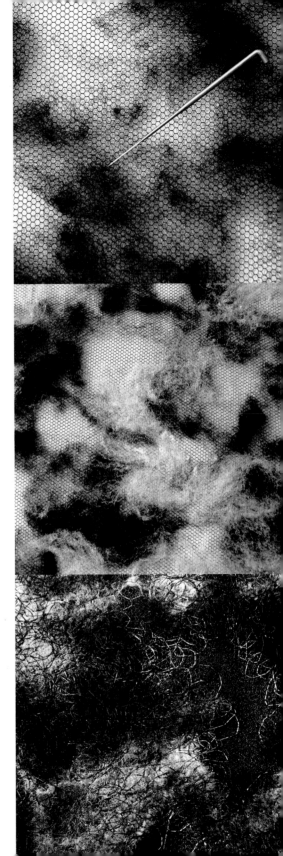

Dark clouds gather (previous pages)
(Cumulus and stratocumulus stratiformis)

Here is a simpler version of the previous technique. The finished textile is opaque rather than lacy. It is done with two yarns of different weights arranged over a fine grey base fabric that is heat-sealing. Cover with greaseproof paper and iron. Finish by partially machine needle felting on both sides to strengthen the textile.

This technique would look good on a fitted waistcoat or jacket.

The oncoming storm
(Stratocumulus opacus)

1 – Using black mesh as a base, tuft with black wool fibre.
2 – Repeat with a paler shade of wool.
3 – Use a sewing machine to embroider swirling lines, adding detail to the design and making it more dense.

Overleaf:
Lightning streaks the sky. This would make an interesting subject because it combines soft, swirling cloudy shapes with the striking graphic qualities of the lightning.

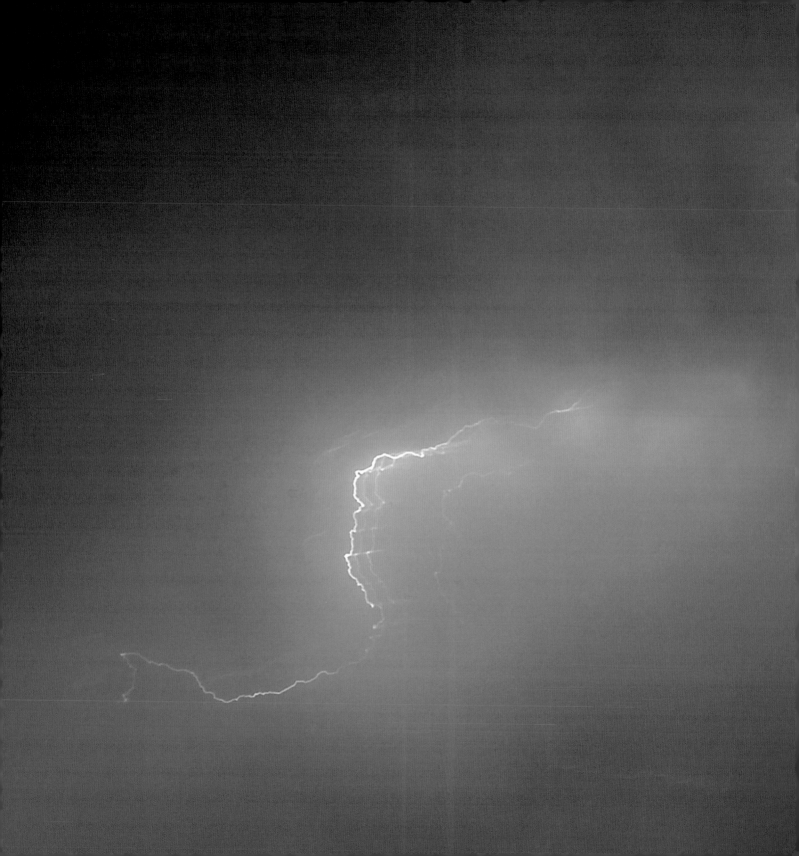

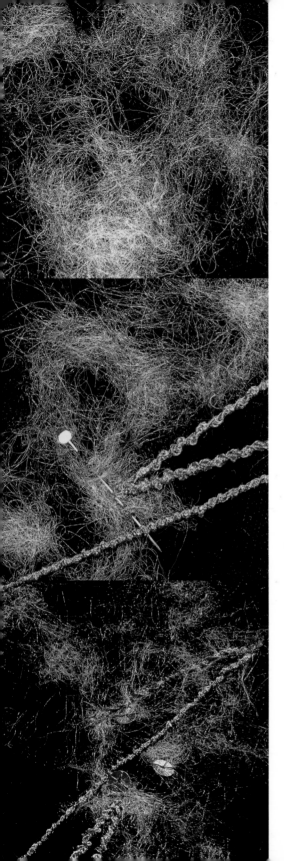

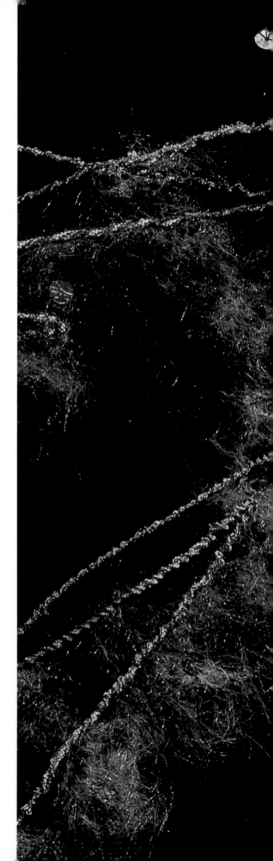

Velvet sky

Try this technique (as shown overleaf)
then experiment with your own versions.

Velvet sky (previous pages)

1 – Use a dark velvet ground – deep brown, navy, indigo or black – and tuft it with synthetic fibres in a range of shades. A fancy fluffy yarn would be ideal for this. Turn the fabric right side up and place it in an embroidery frame.

2 – Arrange metallic yarn in a dynamic pattern and pin in place.

3 – Fix yarn by couching with a thread that matches the background, and add extra sparkle by scattering over some coloured sequins.

This could be used as both a single or an all-over motif, and in a range of different sizes.

Riders on the storm
(Cumulus fractus with altostratus opacus behind)

Here the base is a striped knit in bouclé yarn. The fabric is also lightly felted, so it can be cut without fraying.

1 – Cut strips around 10 mm (½ in.) wide.

2 – Twist and pin them to the base, then fix with couching. Build up areas of texture.

3 – Then take black and white wool fibre and needle felt it to the base by hand, to connect the flat and textured areas of the textile together.

This technique would make a striking waistcoat, or perhaps a bag or purse.

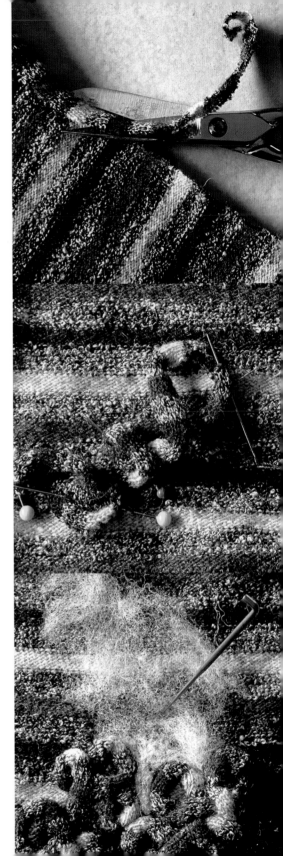

Riders on the storm

(see previous pages)

Heavy with rain
(Cumulus and stratocumulus)

On a base of brushed wool, freely embroider
in raised satin stitch using a woollen yarn.
To increase the relief effect, the first layer of
stitches go in one direction and then a second
layer is added, running perpendicular to the first.
A third layer could also be added where desired.

This could be used decorate a heavy check
or all-over motif, with the embroidered details
scattered freely, forming clusters and spaces.

Dark and stormy

(see overleaf)

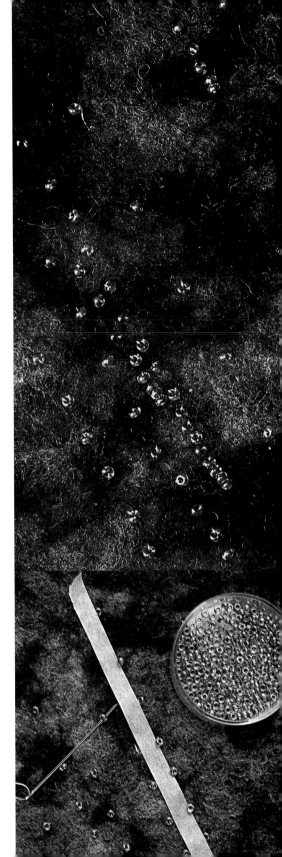

Dark and stormy (previous pages)
(Cumulus and stratocumulus)

The support is a lightly tufted fur fabric, which has been softened by needle felting (see page 37). The clouds are irregular shapes cut from a fairly thick wool fleece. Run a gathering stitch around their edges, gather them up, tie off the thread and then fix them to the background using an appliqué stitch.

This type of textile would work best as an oversized cushion cover or a rug. It could also be used as a decorative motif on a coat.

Scattered raindrops

It's difficult to capture raindrops in a photograph. When the background contains a range of colours, you can see that the highlights look brighter on a dark ground and the shadows look deeper on a pale ground.

This is a piece of hand felting that includes several shades of black and grey in a swirling composition. To create the raindrops, use a craft knife to cut strips of sticky tape, 5 mm (¼ in.) wide. Place the felt inside an embroidery frame and apply the strips of tape in parallel, diagonal lines. Stitch on tiny beads in rows, using the edges of the tape as a guide. To evoke the movement of the raindrops, the distances between the beads can be made wider or narrower.

Rainstorm

1 – Knit a very loose single jersey in a pure wool slub yarn, purling 2 or 3 stitches between each knit stitch and dropping them on the next row. Another way to create this effect is with the technique known as openwork knitting: finish the piece of knitting and then drop every second stitch (or third stitch, or more) and allow it to ladder or run.

2 – By hand, needle felt on both sides in some places, allowing the colours of the yarn to guide you.

3 – Wet felt the fabric and allow it to dry.

4 – Next, using this textile as a base, take a mercerized cotton thread in graduating shades of grey, and embroider running stitch lines, varying the line lengths and spacing.

This could be adapted to make a cosy winter jacket.

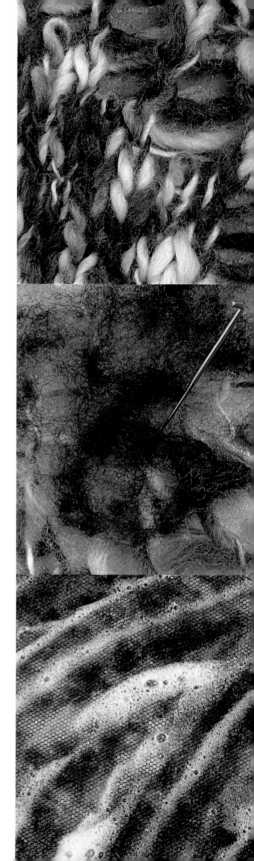

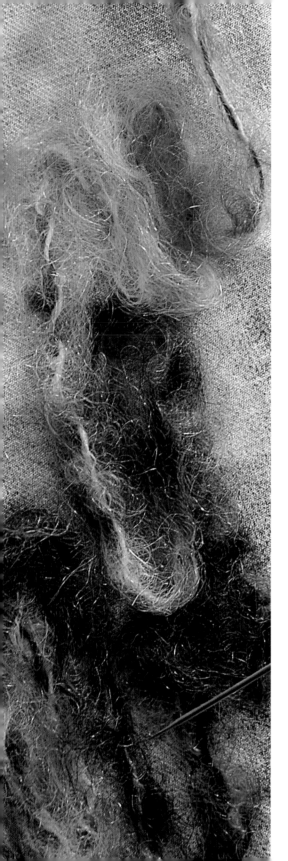

Through the haze

Sometimes the rain can fall so hard that everything becomes a blur. This fake fur effect is actually done by hand tufting.

1 – Use a thick mohair yarn in graduating shades and tuft it through a base of printed cotton.

2 – Briskly brush the pile on the right side, making the fibres lie flat and straight. Finish by ironing under a damp cloth and then brushing once again. You could also apply a fine non-woven to the reverse.

Bringing 'winter' and 'summer' textiles together in this way creates a warm new fabric with a soft and silky feel.

Rain against the windows (overleaf)

This is multicoloured mohair yarn, needle felted by hand onto a cotton print. This creates strong graphic lines and can be adapted by using different types of yarn. Depending on the intended use of the textile, the yarn could be simply needle felted, or fixed down more firmly with couching stitches.

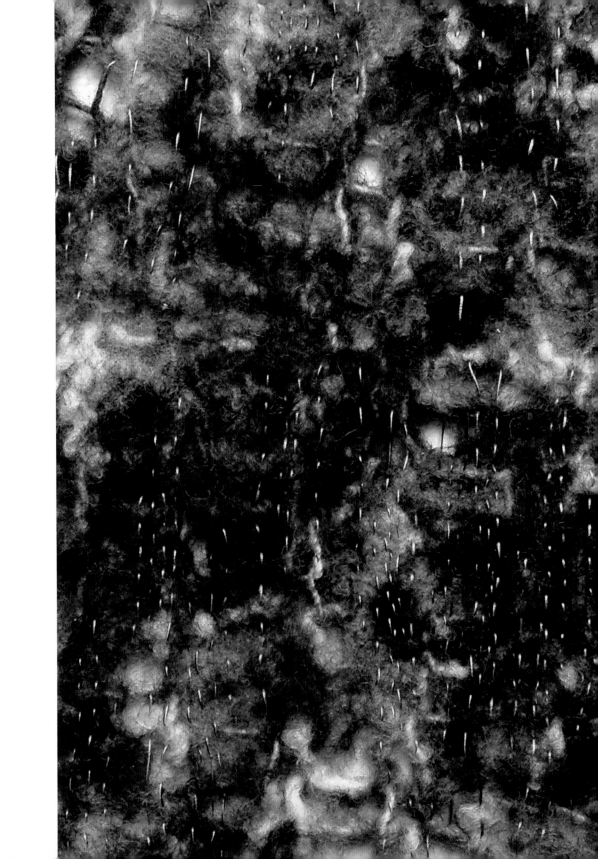

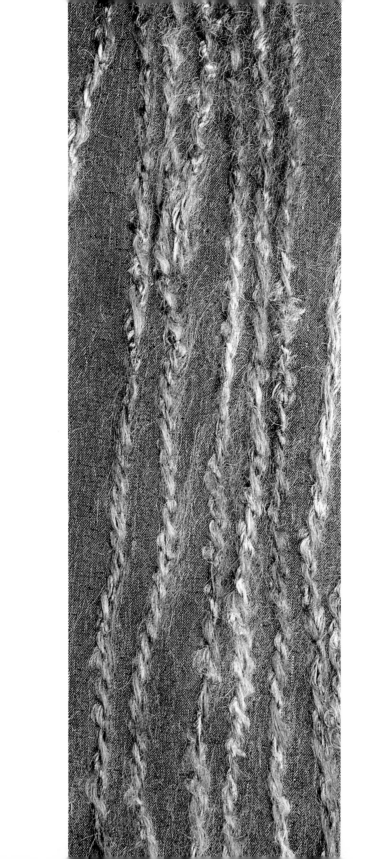

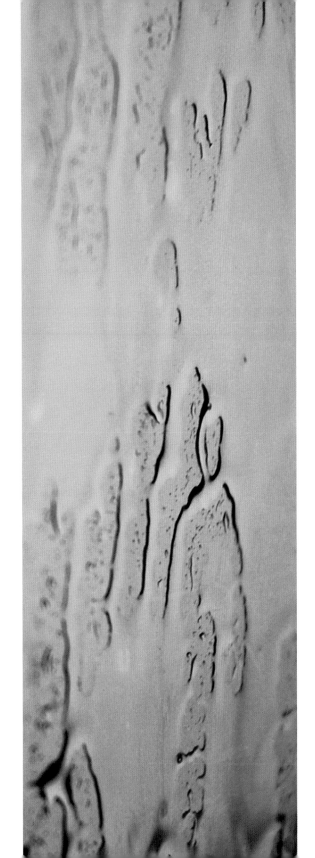

Rain against the windows

(see previous pages)

The sky begins to clear

The base for this textile is a loose knit using fine wire, made either by hand or by machine. This mesh is then carefully needle felted on both sides with different shades of fibre in a random pattern.

The same type of metallic base could be used to create a range of three-dimensional objects, such as lampshades.

The sun shines through (overleaf)

This is a lace fabric needle felted by hand on both sides with black and pale grey wool. Work freely, covering up the underlying lace pattern if desired. This would make a striking scarf or shawl.

The sun shines through
(see previous pages)

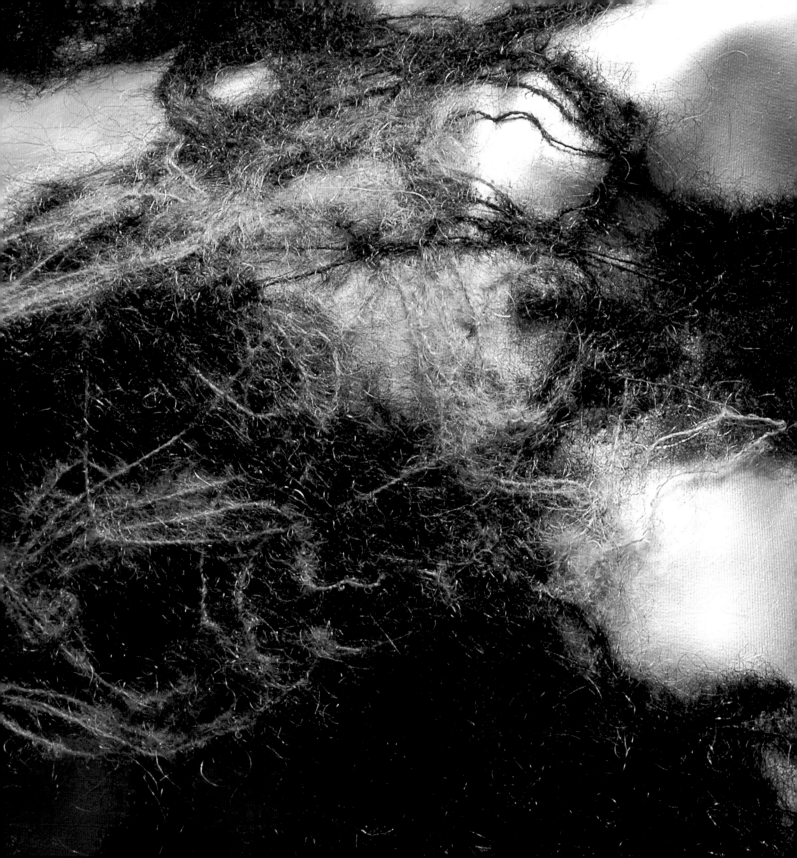

A beam through the darkness

Black wool fibre and fine mohair yarn in black
and grey are needle felted by hand, working
on a soluble non-woven base or simply on a
protective foam layer, to create an arrangement
of dense and empty spaces with intermediate
areas between. Next, position this fine lacy
fabric over a firmer textile in metallic silver.
Use couching to discreetly fix down both the full
areas and the fine threads. This delicate textile
would make an attractive bag or perhaps a jacket.

The haze and rain begin to clear away.

Bright spell

Run a winding row of gathering stitches across a piece of printed net fabric. Pull on the thread to gather the fabric in an irregular pattern, fixing the folds as desired with a few stitches. Then needle felt the folds from both sides, choosing colours to achieve a matching or constrasting effect. You could add a few discreet stitches to fix when finished. The completed textile would make a stunning low-cut top.

Overleaf:
Stratus clouds with the sun shining hazily through.

Altocumulus and stratocumulus

It can be worthwhile to occasionally buy a ball of fancy yarn just so you can rediscover it later and experiment with it. Here it has been applied to the edge of a wool fabric with couching stitches, to form a row of crazy curves.

Added cloudy details are needle felted onto both sides, using a matching shade of wool. These are fixed down with a few stitches.

This edging could be adapted to work on a coat or a throw.

Waves of cloud (pages 172–173)
(Altocumulus stratiformis undulatus)

This technique is almost the same as the one used to create the 'rainstorm' effect on pages 150–151, but the colours and materials are very different.

1 – The openwork knit base is made on a home knitting machine using a fine mohair yarn and a 'magic' bonding yarn.

2 – Place this knit between two layers of greaseproof paper and iron. The bonding yarn will melt and disappear, causing the mohair fibres to stick together. This alows you to form shapes and waves in the knit, especially along the edges.

An alternative to the bonding yarn would be to use an iron-on adhesive fabric that would also almost completely disappear.

3 – By hand, add some needle felted clouds of wool fibre in different colours and iron once again.

This textile would make a feather-light scarf or could be made in shaped pieces and turned into lovely garments that require no sewing. As an additional decoration or tie, fancy yarn in subtle shades (mohair and viscose) can be wet felted by washing machine and applied.

Vertical streaks (pages 174–175)

These amazing patterns are formed by a phenomenon called virgas. Virgas are showers of ice crystals that do not reach the ground. The vapour trail of a plane adds another point of interest to the scene. The composition of coloured wool fibres that have been wet felted by hand is the fruit of experimentation to obtain specific effects. The shapes of paler wool were much lighter and looser to begin with, but felting has turned them into dense cloud formations that no longer resemble the source image, although they are still interesting. Why not experiment and see if you can get closer to the light, streaky effect of virgas yourself?

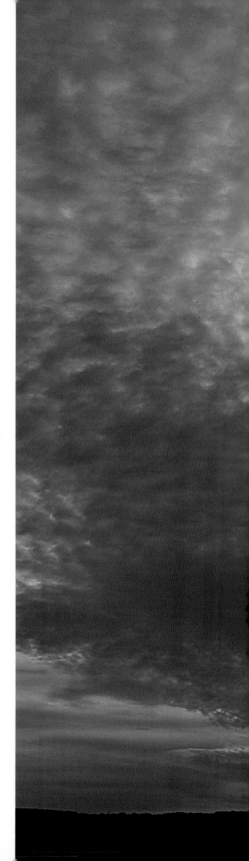

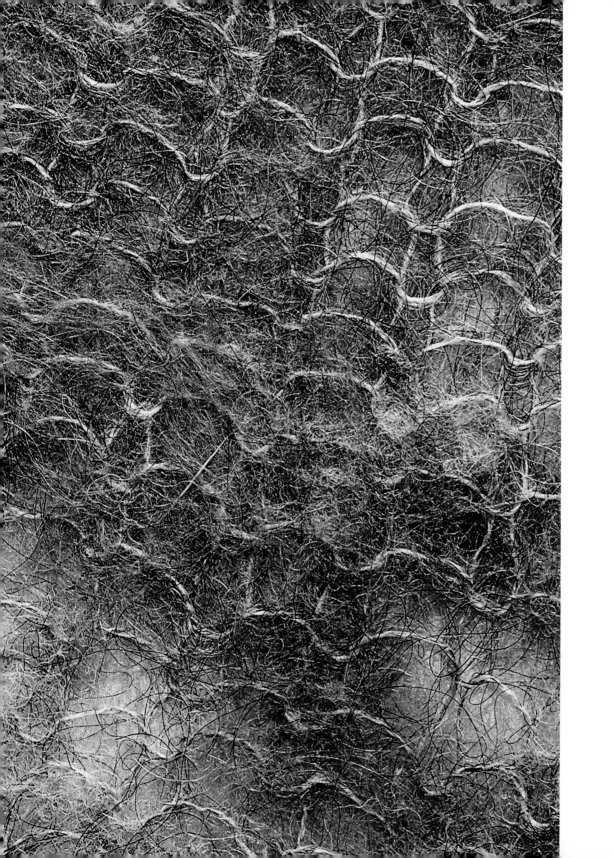

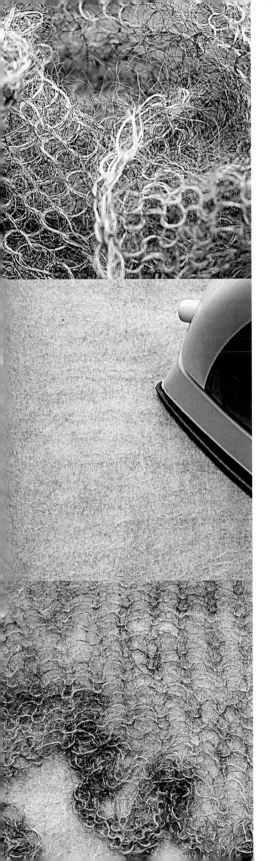

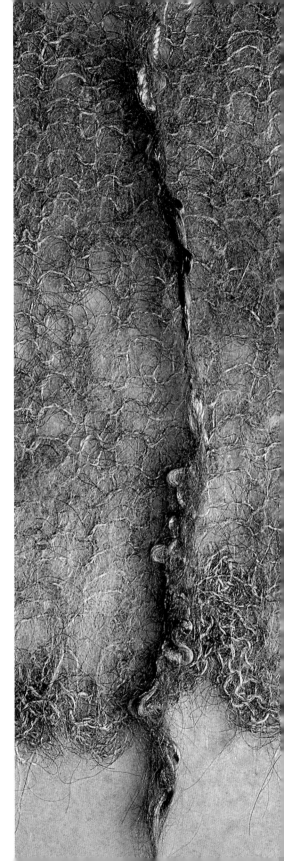

Waves of cloud

(Altocumulus stratiformis undulatus)

Knit an openwork base using a fine mohair
yarn and a bonding yarn.
Place this knit between two layers of
greaseproof paper and iron.
Another option would be to use an ultra-fine
self-adhesive bonding fabric.
Needle felt in a freely worked style.
Finish by felting on some fancy yarn.

Vertical streaks
(see page 170)

Flecks of gold

(see overleaf)

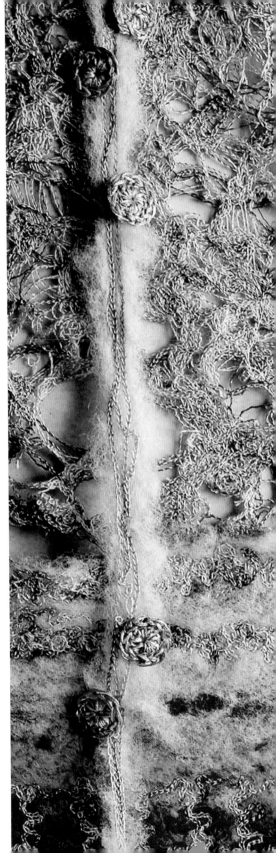

Flecks of gold (pages 176–179)
(Stratocumulus)

Embroidered details are the ideal way to emulate this striking natural pattern.

• The base is wet felted by hand in different colours of wool, with the composition layered to give a pale graduated border on one edge. Chain stitch embroidery with a fancy viscose yarn is used to highlight the design. Try this on a jacket or for small objects such as purses and bags.

• The jewel-like chains are made by needle felting some long thin strands of wool. Then thread a needle with wire thread and slide it through the strand, working a long chain stitch. The little 'sun' motifs are crocheted, using a combination of sewing and embroidery yarns (5, 6 or 7 in viscose or cotton, with an additional gold lurex thread) in either a single colour or graduated shades for a multi-tone effect. Use a fine steel crochet hook: chain 3 and stitch into the first stitch; chain 3 again, 10 ½ stitches into the centre, then close. Finish the threads with a needle and cut off any excess. To make the discs stiffer and stronger, put a drop of fixative on the back of each one.

Misty sunset

The base for this atmospheric piece is a lace fabric made by machine embroidering on a soluble non-woven. You could accentuate the contrast between night and day by highlighting other oppositions, such as density and space, warmth and cold, delicacy and heaviness.

The lace is then used as a base for felting. Wool fibre is arranged in fine, uneven layers on both sides and the fabric is then wet felted by hand (see pages 22, 190 and 228).

Overleaf:
Sunset with altocumulus and cirrus fibratus.

Plumes of beauty

Cut some small pieces of bouclé yarn: a multicoloured twist would be particularly suitable for this. You could also make a yarn by twisting several different kinds of thread together. Next, needle felt by hand onto a base of grey wool, allowing the yarn to form lines and curves. Any mistakes can easily be rectified by gently pulling out the unwanted fibres. Depending on the results you want, couching stitches could be used to fix down the yarn. This motif would give a heavenly touch to a wide range of clothes and fashion accessories.

Overleaf:
A wild sunset sky.

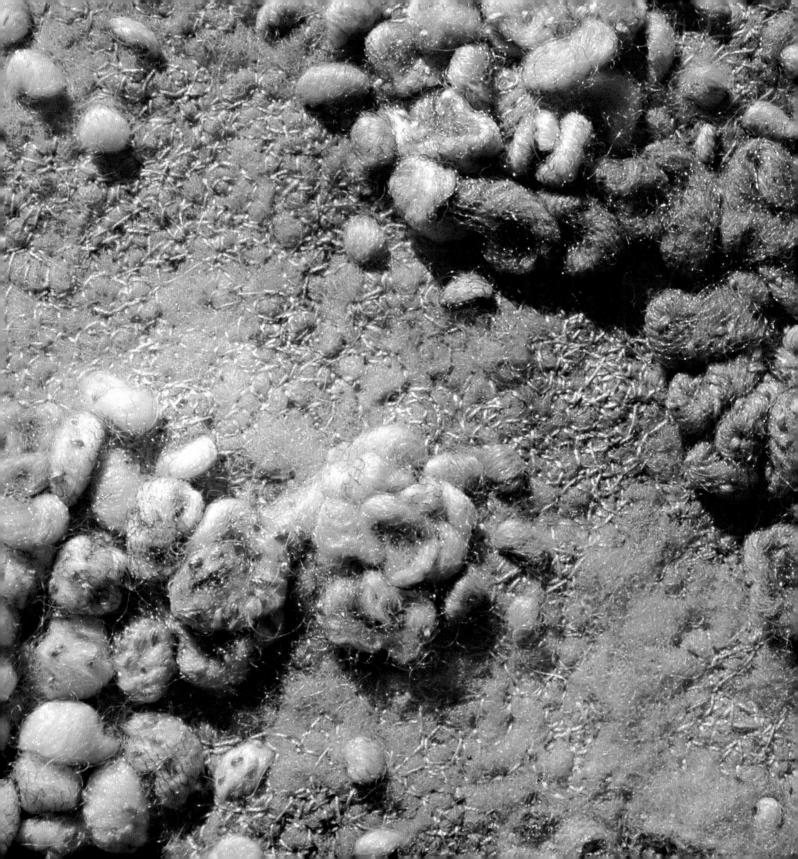

Sunset shades

1 – Create the base fabric by wet felting by hand, using a range of pastel colours: greys, pinks and blues. Leave it to dry.

2 – Next you will need an irregular yarn in graduating colours, and a special tubular nylon tape, available from specialist haberdashery suppliers. Fix a small safety pin to one end of the coloured yarn and feed it through the nylon tubing.

3 – Freely work machine embroidery over the felt base, building up a random composition. Then apply the coloured piping that you have made to the surface with couching stitches, building up a pattern of tight curls of varying sizes and depths.

Finish by embroidering some bright highlights by hand, using straight stitch in orange and yellow embroidery yarn.

Textured waves (overleaf)
(Altocumulus floccus, altocumulus and altostratus opacus)

Using carded wool in a variety of shades, entirely cover the reverse side of a piece of lurex lace. Scatter a few touches of pink on the right side. Then wet felt, preferably by hand.

Textured waves
(see previous pages)

As evening falls

This wet felt is made with carded wool in beige, pale pink, peach, grey and black, with the colours graduating and fading out into the border. Delicate grey-blues and pinks with a hint of black would make a lovely baby gift, such as a blanket for a pushchair.

Evanescence (pages 196–197)
(Altocumulus floccus)

Another experiment with wet felting in graduated tones. This time the colours used are pink, blue, grey, orange and pale yellow.

Overleaf:
Nimbostratus clouds.

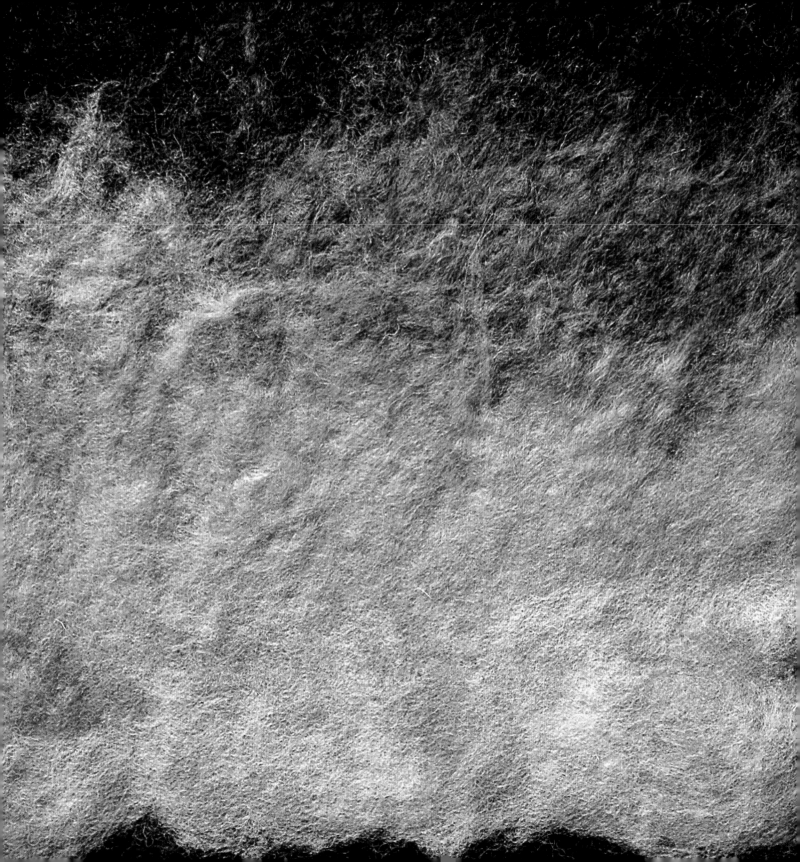

Evanescence
(see page 192)

Clouds on fire
(Cumulus congestus)

This felt succeeds in closely replicating the delicate blue and pink colouration seen in the images opposite and on the previous pages, but the design still has an appealing abstract quality. It would enliven the edging of a coat or blanket, either in these tones or in another colourway.

Daubs and depth

The base is produced by wet felting with a fancy yarn. The textured pieces are made of wool fabric that has been deliberately worn down by needle felting. These are then stitched to the background and allowed to curl naturally.

The weight of clouds (overleaf)

Despite their apparent lightness, it is well-known that clouds are in fact very heavy and can weigh thousands of tons!

This effect is done by hand tufting on a base of mesh. The work is done from the reverse side: the felting needle pulls the fibres through the mesh and into the protective foam. Use a range of yarns in different materials to vary the effects, colours and textures. Pull the textile off the foam base and fix a layer of iron-on adhesive film onto the back to strengthen the piece.

The weight of clouds
(see previous pages)

A Fauvist sky
(Cumulus fractus)

Here's another composition made in the same way, this time on a cotton base. As on the previous pages, it could be finished by applying an iron-on non-woven to the reverse. Use this technique to brighten up any fashion item or to make cushions and bags.

Square clouds at twilight (overleaf)
(Cumulus fractus and humilis)

Geometric shapes are not usually found in the sky, so this is something of an artistic exaggeration. This textile is made with wool that is lightly needle felted by hand to form the basic motifs and then wet felted. Like any soft felt, it could be used for shawls, scarfs, tops, blankets and throws.

Multicoloured cumulus (pages 210–211)

This textile is made in the same way as the previous one. If you like the look of these colour effects, why not try creating similar textiles on a larger scale?

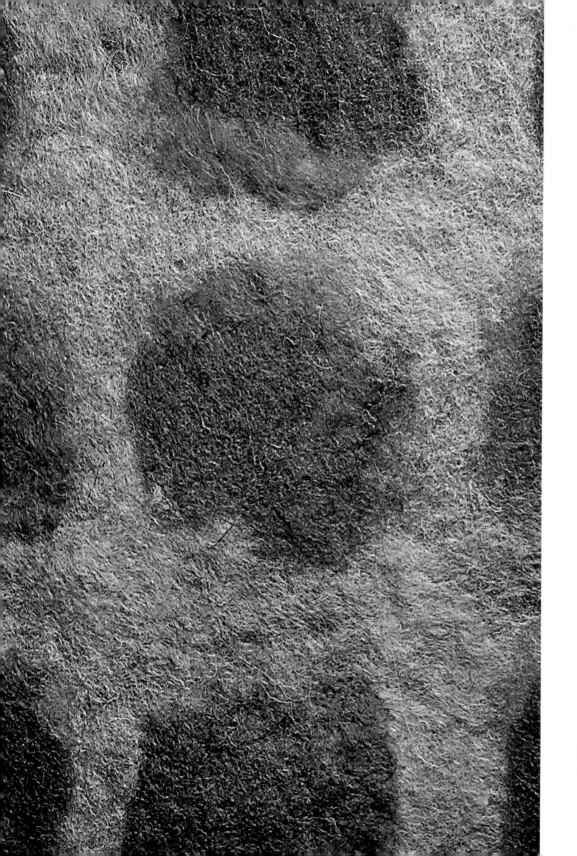

Square clouds at twilight

(see previous page)

Multicoloured cumulus

(see page 207)

A fantasy sky

(see overleaf)

A fantasy sky (previous pages)

Here is a chance to experiment with a range of thick wool yarns in a striking range of flame-like colours and textures. They make a great subject for needle felting on a soluble non-woven base. Arrange the different colours in a fairly dense pattern, letting your imagination run free. Begin by needle felting the places where the colours cross, and then the rest of the area, either by hand or by machine. It's up to you to choose which is the right side, depending on whether you want a flat effect or more texture and depth. With a little creativity, this could be turned into a striking scarf or top.

Blazing sunset
(Cirrus, altocumulus and stratocumulus)

You can make your own knitting yarn using wool fibre in various colours. This method is only for the extremely dedicated. Pull off small pieces of fibre, preferably long and thin, and roll them between your fingers to a diameter of 7 to 10 mm (¼ to ½ in.). Join them together by overlapping the ends and change colours regularly, depending on the effect you want.

You could also use a fine or medium knitting yarn as a base and needle felt coloured fibres along its length. This takes longer but gives a more solid result. Roll the yarn into a ball.

1 – Choose thick knitting needles for this yarn. Cast on and knit in stocking stitch or garter stitch.

2 – Wet felt the fabric lightly to make the texture fuzzier and also to strengthen the twisted yarn.

3 – Next, cut out strips of shot silk, about 1 cm (½ in.) wide. Fray the edges and tack onto the felted knit, then stitch by hand or by machine. Try this effect for fashion or home accessories.

Sunset stripes (overleaf)
(Cirrus spissatus)

Wool fibres in orange, red and pink are needle felted into a grey base of fleece or brushed woollen. Then, to emphasize the contrast between sharp and blurred lines, two or three lengths of fine mohair yarn are carefully placed over the stripes and needle felted. Why not try brightening up an old scarf or shawl or extending the sleeves of a sweater by needle felting new striped borders in this style?

Sunset stripes

(see previous pages)

Bands of flame

(see overleaf)

Bands of flame (previous pages)
(Cirrostratus)

Before making a needle felted scarf, it's best to have an initial trial run using the same materials, because needle felting (like wet felting) results in heavy shrinkage, both lengthways and widthways. Measure the length of the yarn before making your sample (A) and the length of the finished sample (B). Decide how long you want the finished scarf to be and call that figure C. Then use the following rule of three: the length of the scarf before felting should be equal to A multiplied C, divided by B.

   On a soluble non-woven base, layer a series of different yarns (wool, angora, mohair). Cover with greaseproof paper and iron flat. Then take off the paper and needle felt all over by machine. Add extra yarn to any sparse or flimsy areas and needle felt once again.

A hint of green
(Cirrus and altocumulus)

Green sunshine may seem impossible, but a sunset sky can sometimes take on a greenish hue. These woollen stripes are lightly needle felted by hand and then wet felted in the washing machine.

A beautiful sky is easy to capture in a photograph, but even with practice and patience, it's difficult to achieve the same effect in felt. Nonetheless, a piece that fails to reflect the source image can still provide inspiration and interest.

Layers and motion

1 – Using the wet felting by hand techniques explained on pages 22 and 207, produce a base felt with coloured swirls.

2 – Next, embroider in chain stitch on the wrong side, then to integrate this embroidery, turn the fabric over and use a felting needle to tuft it through in places. This tufting technique allows you to firm up a fabric or adjust a design (see page 57).

3 – For an attractive finish, apply a piece of embroidered guipure lace, made by freely working in chain stitch on a soluble non-woven ground. Wash carefully and allow to dry.

(overleaf)

This guipure in chain-stitch embroidery was made by scattering an irregular pattern of coloured wool fibre on both sides and then wet felting by hand (see page 190).

Previous pages:
Chaotic clouds in a sunset sky.

Crenellated clouds (pages 132–133)
(Cirrus, altocumulus and stratocumulus)

1 – Choose silvery yarns in varying textures, to match the base fabric of shot crushed velvet.

2 – Cut these yarns into pieces of varying lengths and needle felt them to the base, following the lines of the crushed velvet. The design is fluid and frequently broken to reinforce the feeling of light and shade.

3 – Finish by machine needle felting all over. You could also fix down some of the yarn with couching.

For beginners, this would make a great scarf design, while the more experienced and ambitious could attempt a coat or dress. The same technique could also be used to make classy cushion covers for a sophisticated interior.

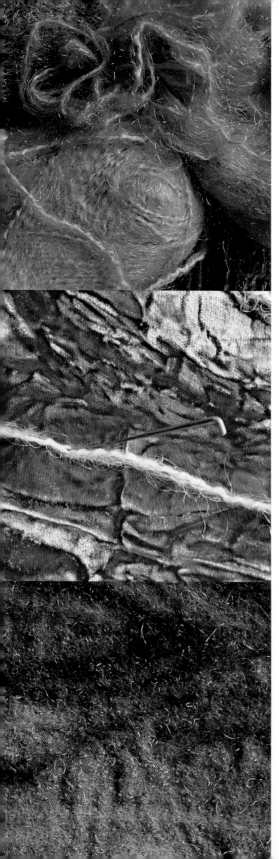

Previous pages:
Cirrus, altocumulus and
stratocumulus clouds at sunset.

Crenellated clouds

(continued)

1 – Select a range of fluffy yarns to
match the velvet base fabric.
2 – Needle felt on the right side,
following the flowing lines of the support.
3 – Finish by machine needle felting on
the reverse, or couching by hand.

A string of glowing clouds
(Cumulus and altocumulus)

To create the crumpled relief of this edging,
thread your sewing machine with elastic yarn
and sew curving lines on a black jersey ground.
In the hollow areas, needle felt by hand with
wool fibre in glowing colours to evoke clouds
lit by the setting sun. Add a few couching stitches
to fix. This would make a charming border for
a lightweight top.

Previous pages:
Cumulus fractus clouds form a long frieze.

Overleaf:
The last rays of the setting sun, before night falls.

Fireworks (opposite and overleaf)

Begin by tufting the base: use a black fleece knit and create sparks of colour by scattering coloured wool fibre on the reverse side and tufting through with a felting needle. Turn the textile over and brush to mingle the fibres.

Next, embroider bright points of light in detached chain stitch in a range of firework shades: red, orange, emerald green and turquoise.

To accentuate the effect of movement and depth, you could add twists of a suitable fancy yarn, fixing it with couching. You could also make a similar yarn yourself by decorating a light non-woven tape with fabric paints. This would look good on a fleece jacket for a child.

Fireworks

1 – Tuft a base fabric of black fleece with lengths of multicoloured wool.
2 – Brush the right side of the fabric.
3 – Embroider details in detached chain stitch and use fabric glue to apply a fancy yarn and fix with couching.

Festival of lights (overleaf)

Like the piece on page 240, this is made using the tufting technique. The base is a fine fleecy knit in bright red.

1 – Cover the reverse in a variety of multicoloured wool fibres: cream, yellow, turquoise, deep blue. Tuft through.

2 – View of the right side.

3 – Strengthen the piece by applying iron-on film to the reverse.

4 – Turn to the right side and add embroidered details in straight stitch, using mercerized or silk-finish yarn in red, blue, pink and yellow.

This makes a great all-over motif, or could be used as an individual motif on a fleece jacket, for example.

Previous pages:
A shower of shimmering sparks.

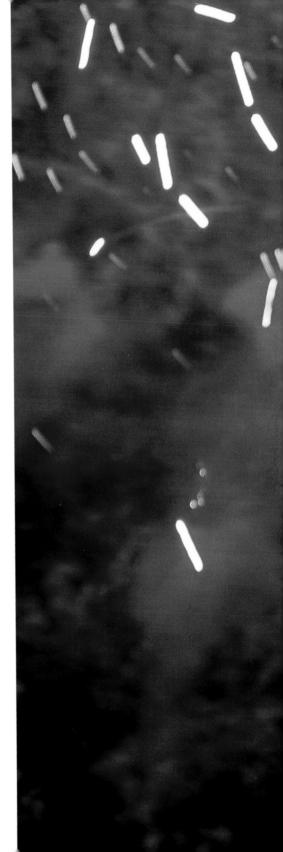

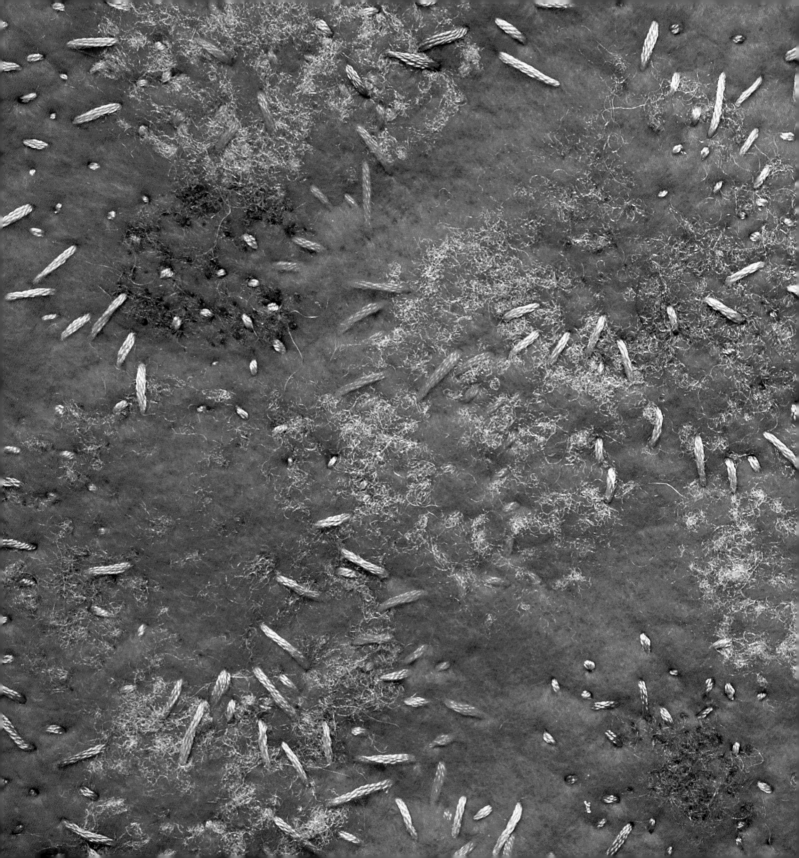

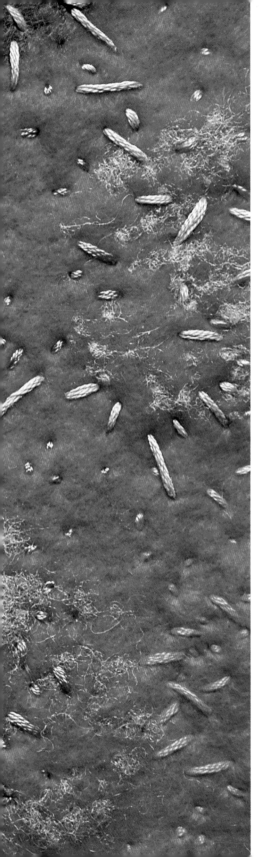

Festival of lights

(continued)

1 – Use a fleece base, use tufting to create bursts of different colours.
2 – View of the right side.
3 – Iron a non-woven film onto the reverse. Embroider flying sparks in straight stitch, as shown on the left.

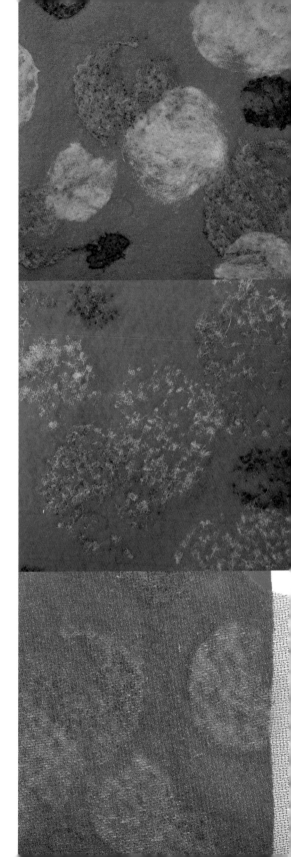

A riot of colours

To create the textile shown on the left, choose a
silk base and cut out small pieces of shot satin in a
matching shade. Fray the edges of the satin pieces,
then scatter them over the base. Pin them in position,
tack with soluble thread, then needle felt by machine.

To create the textile shown opposite, proceed in
the same way but using satin in different colours. You
could do the needle felting by hand, but if so, it's best
to use couching stitches to fix the finer details.

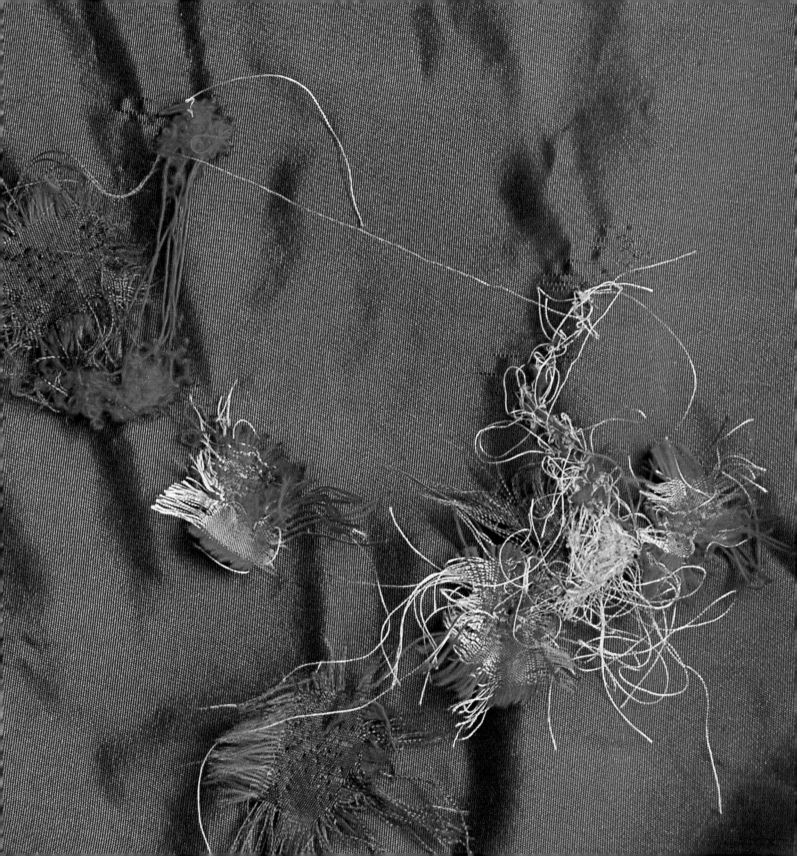

A sky full of sparks

(see overleaf)

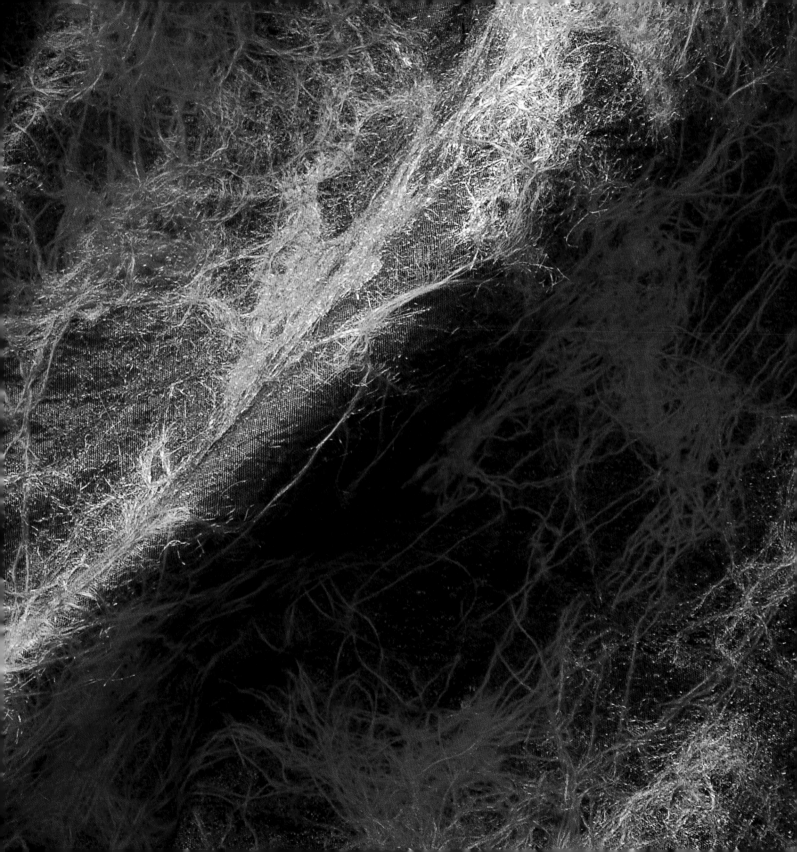

A sky full of sparks (previous pages)

The clouds of sparks are created by machine needle felting all the frayed threads from the edges of a shot silk base. This produces a reversible textile that makes an excellent scarf or shawl.

Shimmering moonlight (pages 256–259)

The background fabric here is a black wool and silver lurex knit. Needle felt wool fibre onto a soluble non-woven base. Using a hole-punch and a hammer, punch out circles and rings of different sizes. Arrange these on the lurex knit, pin and tack with soluble thread, and needle felt to fix. Finally, wash to remove the non-woven and the thread.

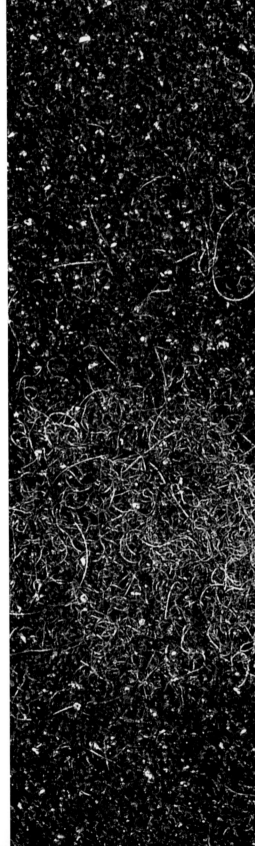

Shimmering moonlight

(see previous page and overleaf)

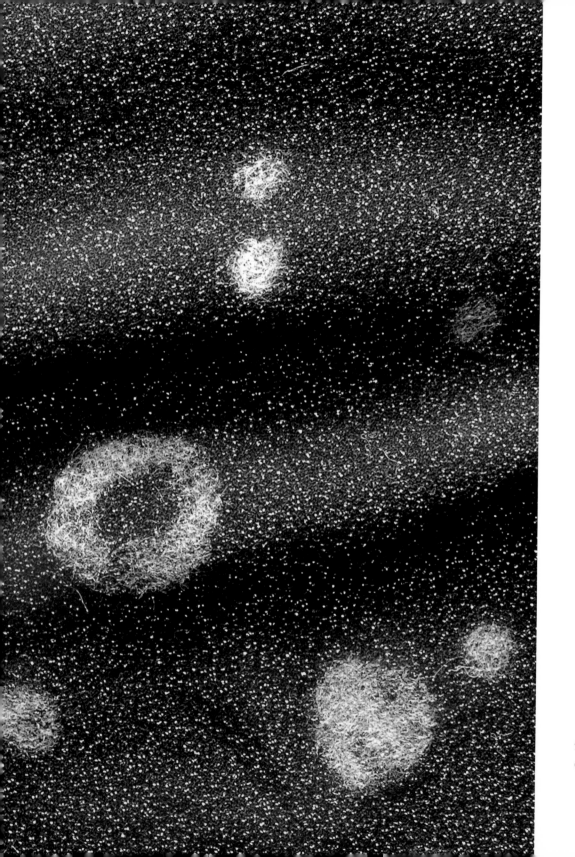

Shimmering moonlight
(see page 255)

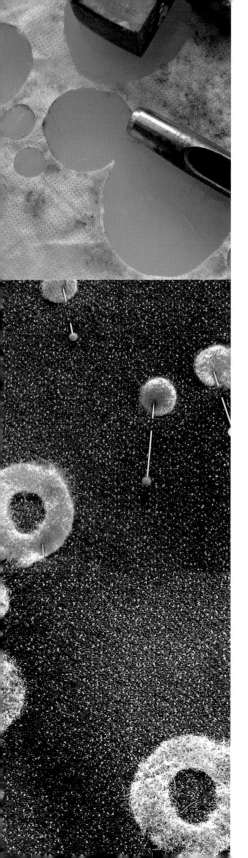

Twilight rays (overleaf)

Scatter a chiffon base (see pages 122 and 123) with wool fibre in various colours. Then place between two layers of cloth to hold the fibres in place. Pin together and then tack all over with large stitches. Wet felt in a washing machine at 35–40 °C.

When the machine has finished, take out the felt, unpick the tacking and remove the protective layers. The wool fibres will be firmly fixed to the base and the chiffon will have shrunk, forming puckered creases. This type of fabric makes a good scarf or blouse, and can also be used as a base for other effects.

Moon and stars (page 263)

Layer wool fibre in different colours, beginning with black and navy blue, then working towards paler colours like yellow and beige. Lightly needle felt the whole area and concentrate on individual spots to create bright 'stars' on the darker side of the fabric. Sandwich in linen and hold together with tacking stitches all over. Wet felt in a washing machine at 40 °C.

Twilight rays

(see previous page)

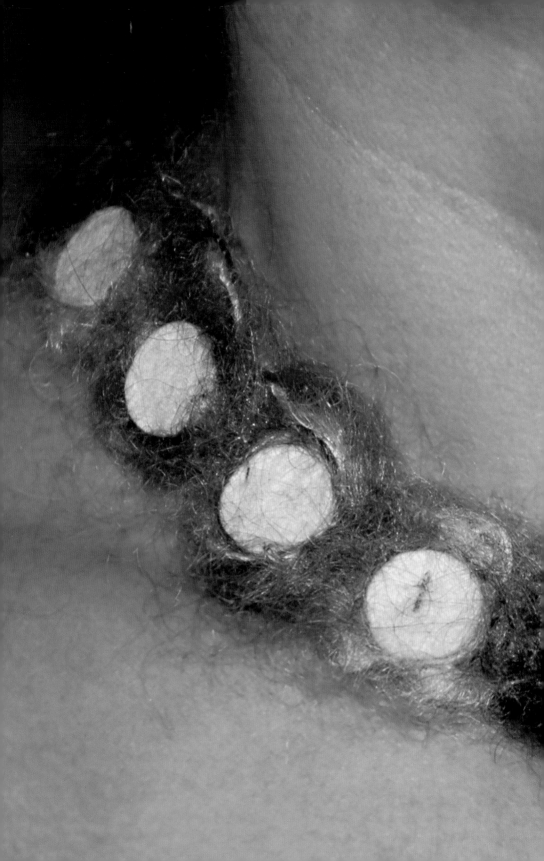

When the machine has finished, unpick the tacking and let the textile dry. If you like the results, why not think about possible uses for the same design in different sizes, perhaps for a purse or a bag? A soft, light and reversible fabric might inspire you to make a scarf, which would be an easy shape to start with.

Clouds across the moon

This necklace is made of felt discs, each one wrapped in a brushed and printed mohair yarn which is fixed with couching. Measure it around your neck to get the length right and fix on a fastener. If you have no ready-made felt discs, you could make them yourself. Roll wool fibre into a sausage shape, needle felt it and then wet felt it by hand (see page 22) by rolling and unrolling it inside a straw mat. When the felt roll is compact and firm, it can be cut into rounds with a craft knife.

By using multicoloured wool fibre for the discs, you can also create attractive concentric designs. Experiment and see what effects you can achieve.

Overleaf:
The rising sun.

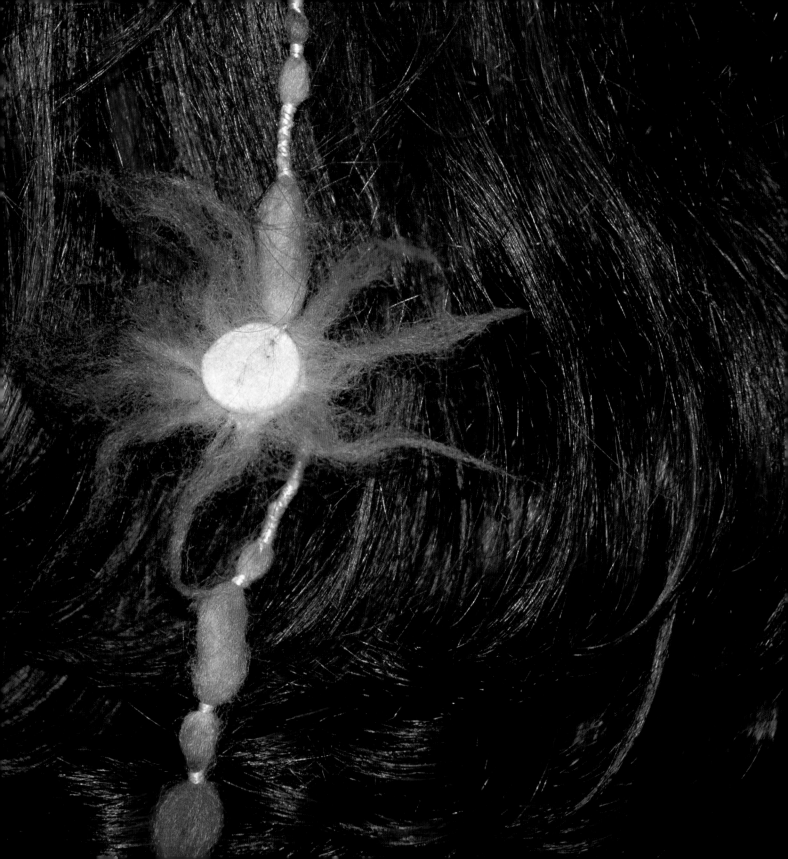

Dawn sunburst

(see overleaf)

Dawn sunburst (previous pages)

For this project you will need an attractive fancy yarn, or you could dye some wool fibre yourself. Cut short pieces of yarn, 5 or 6 cm (2 to 2 ½ in.) long. Then use a hole-punch to cut out two thin discs of craft felt, 1 cm (½ in.) across and apply some glue to them. Criss-cross the pieces of wool in a sunburst shape and stick a felt disc on each side. Pin together until the glue is dry, then fray the strands of yarn to make rays. Make more sunbursts in different shades if desired.

Separately, make a long hank of wool fibre, and tie here and there with silky embroidery yarn in a matching shade, to form a braid or tassel. Attach the sunbursts to the tassel, and wear it as a fun hair decoration, a bag charm or a necklace.

Leaving on a jet plane

Passing planes create long vapour trails known as contrails. The aircraft's engines cause the water vapour in the air to condense, creating a stream of tiny ice crystals. A contrail will only form under certain cold and humid conditions, which are generally found at high altitudes. It takes some time for the ice crystals to form behind the plane, and the action of wind can create interesting visual effects.

Bright contrails

Using diluted fabric paints, paint random patches
of colour on a cotton base. Then use wool fibre
and machine needle felting to create long, hazy
lines that criss-cross the base. Try to keep it light
and not overwork the fabric.

The resulting textile (opposite) is
neither light nor heavy, and has a fascinating
texture. It would be great for spring and autumn
clothes and accessories.

Soft contrails

The mohair fabric on the right is machine
needle felted with a multicoloured fancy yarn
(see page 215). Pieces of wool fibre that
resemble brushstrokes are then needle felted
over the top.

Criss-cross trails

This felt is made from cream wool fibre and textured yarn in a range of bright colours. It is then machine embroidered with long diagonals lines in back stitch.

Heat haze (overleaf)

This delicately coloured textile is made by machine felting pastel wool fibres and yarns on a soluble non-woven base. Wash to dissolve the base and allow to dry.

Opposite:
This sky looks like something from
a dramatic comic book scene.

Heat haze

(see previous page)

Soft waves

Prepare several layers of grey wool fibre as a base.
Using a paler shade of fibre, create two or three
diagonal lines, varying the width and opacity.
Then arrange some criss-crossing threads of mohair
yarn in pastel colours. Needle felt lightly by hand to
keep the yarns in place, then wet felt either by hand
or machine. This would make a lovely scarf.

Overleaf:
A blurred pattern of contrails.

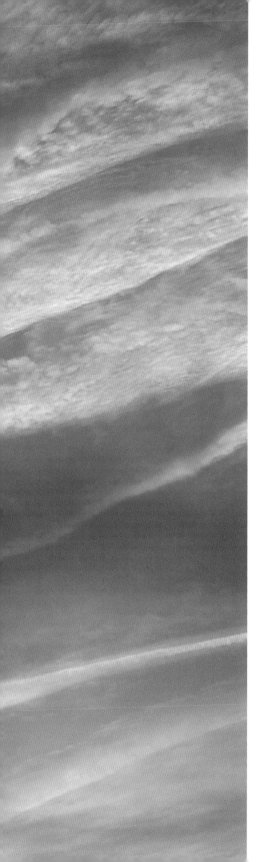

Snowy white rows

(see overleaf)

283

Snowy white rows

Boiled wool is a felted fabric that is readily available in stores. It is light and supple and, like all felts, has the advantage that it can be cut to shape and will not fray or unravel. This warm wrap needs a base that measures approximately 2 m (6 feet) by 40 cm (15 in.). If the fabric isn't wide enough, you could sew two or more pieces together; it won't show.

1 – To make the first pleat, fold the fabric longways around 1.5 to 2.5 cm (¾ to 1 in.) from the edge. Machine stitch as close to the selvedge as possible.
2 – Repeat this process across the fabric, leaving a space of around 1.5 to 2.5 cm (¾ to 1 in.) between the pleats. You could keep the heights of the pleats even or create variations. You could even vary the height of a single pleat across its length.
3 – When you have finished stitching the pleats, use a craft knife to cut each pleat into parallel bands, 3 mm (⅛ in.) away from the row of stitches. Hem each edge of the scarf if desired.

Cloudlike loops look effective in wavy rows (**left**) and also in a more freeform composition (**opposite**).

Clouds beneath your feet (previous pages, left)

This rug is made in the same way as the wrap on page 283, using a felt 3 mm (⅛ in.) thick. The heights of the loops range from 1 to 3 cm (½ to 1 ½ in.).

Swirls and curls

Here are some similar ideas to explore, which move away from the basic concept of straight rows of loops.

Cut out strips of craft felt, about 9 cm (3 ½ in.) wide. Then cut them widthways into two irregular pieces along a wavy line, so that the width of each piece varies between 2.5 and 6.5 cm (1 and 2 ½ in.).

Fold each piece in half and join the edges by machine stitching 2 mm from the edge. To make the fringes, cut parallel slits all along each piece with a craft knife, spacing the slits 5 to 10 mm (¼ to ½ in.) apart and keeping 5 mm (¼ in.) away from the stitched edge.

Use a felt base 3 mm (⅛ in.) thick, in the same colour as the fringes, and couch down the fringed strips so that the loops stand up vertically. You could build up a dense pattern at random (see previous page) or create flower-like twists and curls (opposite).

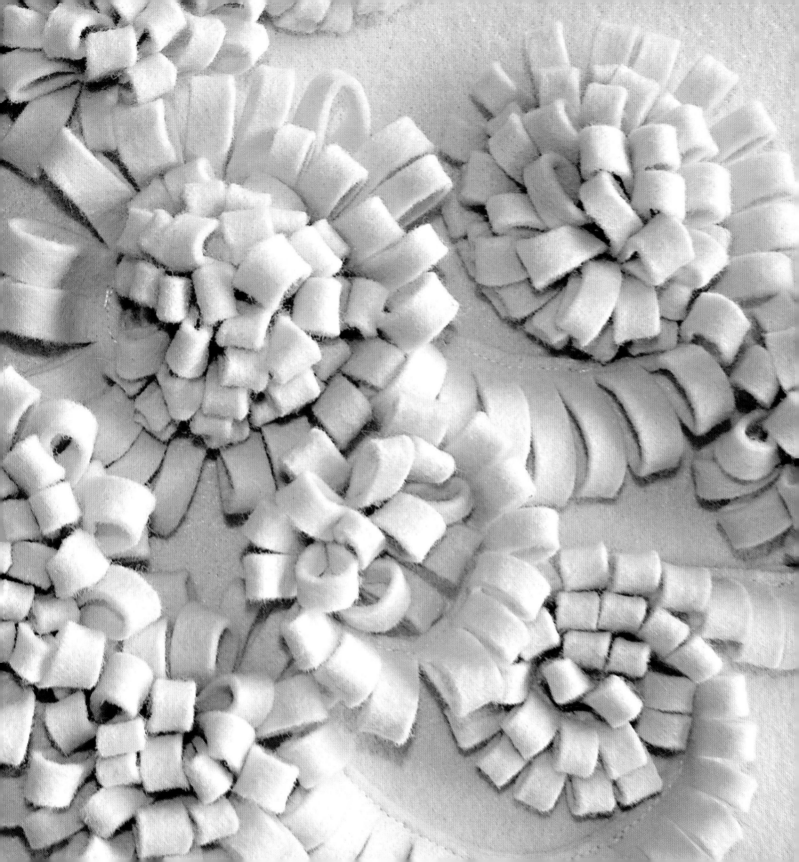

Walking in the air

This textile is made using fur fabric. Needle felting fake fur is easy and fun. It allows you to personalize the fabric by working with its depth and thickness to create flat areas, break up regular patterns, give a sense of movement, or add colour contrasts in the form of wool tufting.

The image on the left shows the fur fabric before needle felting, and right, the finished effect.

Overleaf:
A sea of cumulus clouds seen from a plane.

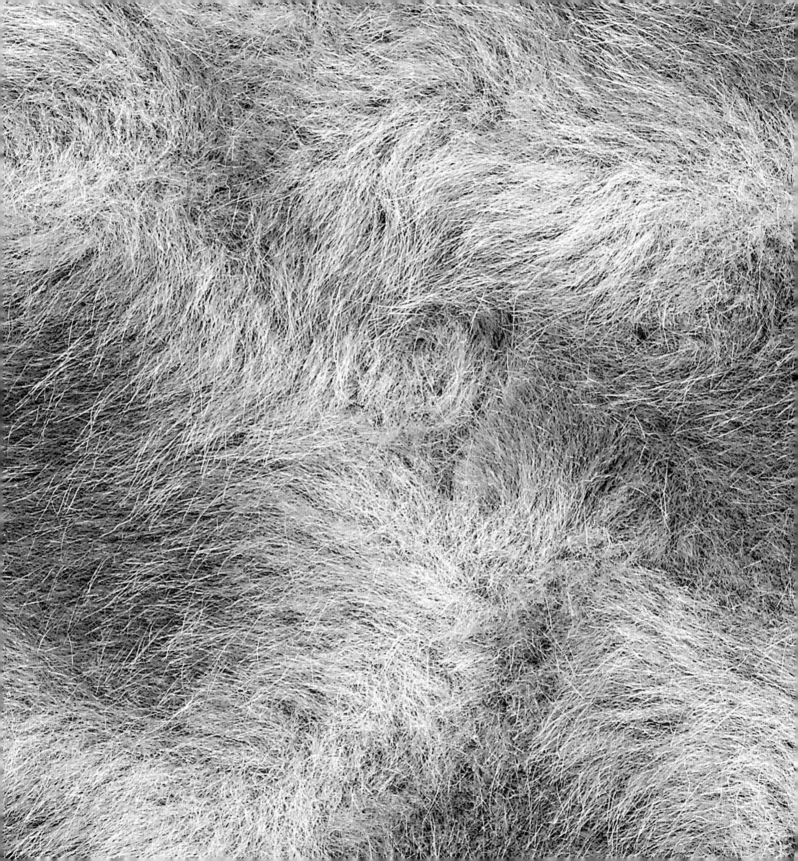

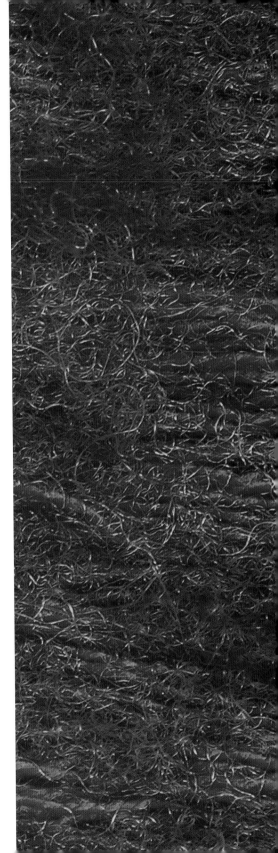

Sky becomes sea (previous pages)
(Altocumulus floccus)

Changing the orientation of an image can create
a totally different look, sparking off new creative
ideas and opening up new horizons.

Dream clouds
(Cirrus and cirrocumulus)

Here are some textiles inspired by the idea
of viewing the world upside down.
• For the brushstroke effect in the top half of the
image opposite: Stretch some cotton threads on
a frame. Cover with wallpaper paste and allow to
dry completely. To make it easier to take them
out of the frame, cut them into two or three
pieces then place them on a protective foam
base and cover with wadding in a contrasting
shade. Needle felt from both sides, incorporating
the threads into the wool, then wet felt lightly by
hand. Wash and allow to dry.
• For the 'sea foam' effect (see overleaf): Craft felt
in several colours is shredded up with a needle
felting machine. The shreds are then arranged in
a scattered pattern over a thin base of iron-on
fabric. Greaseproof paper is then carefully placed
over the top and an iron is used to activate the
glue. The lightness and transparency of this effect
should give you lots of ideas to experiment with.

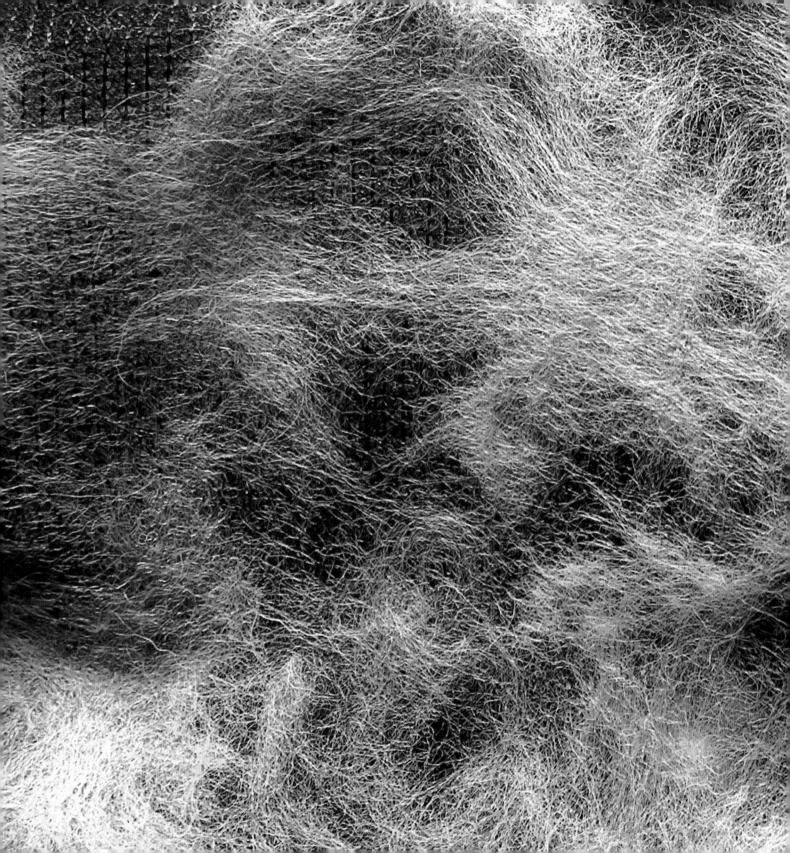

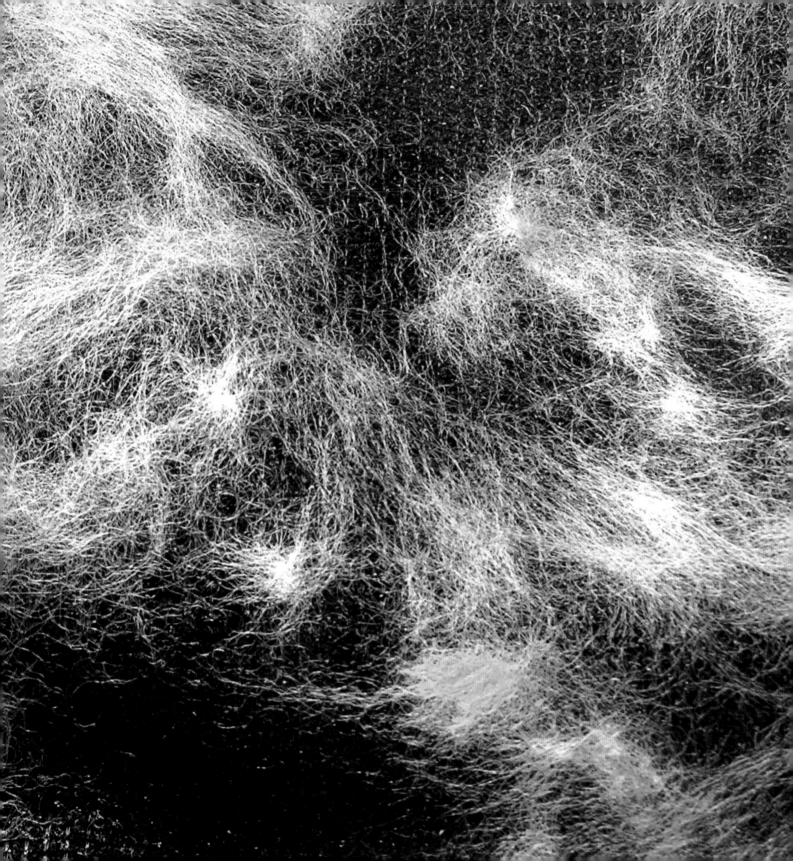

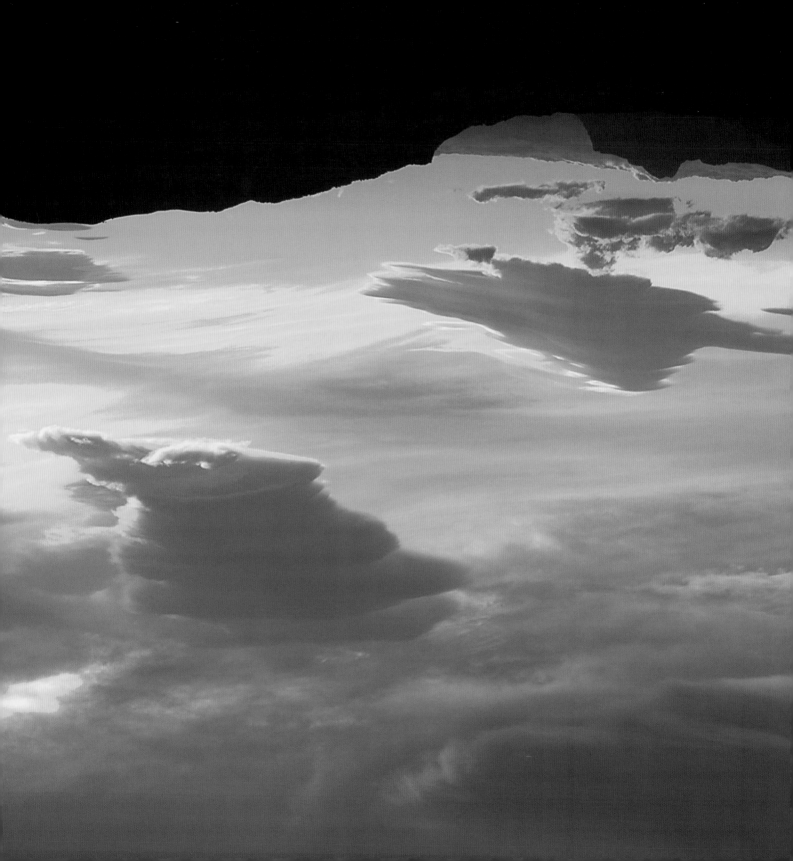

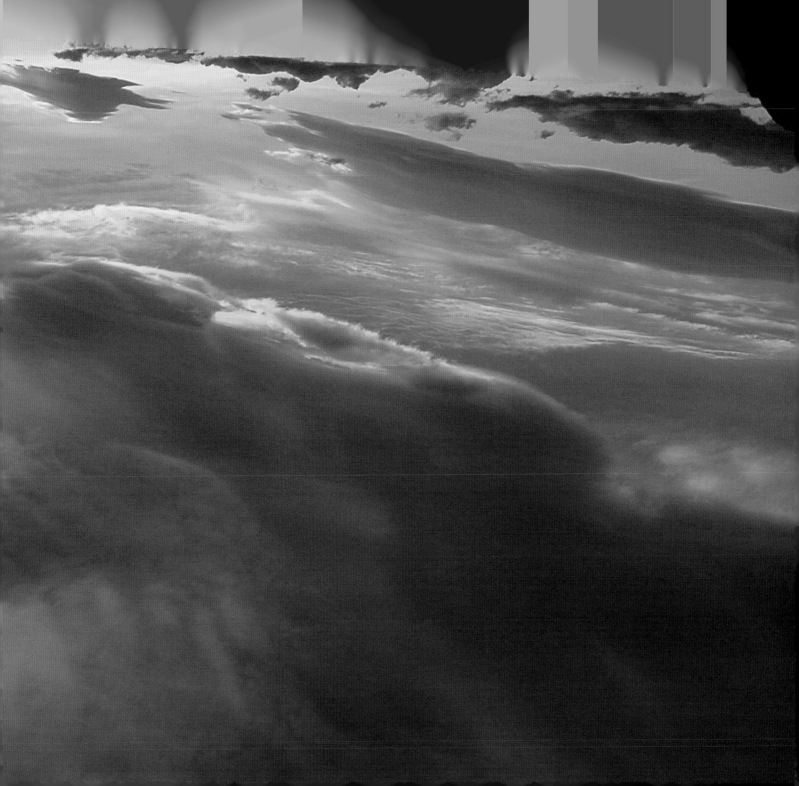

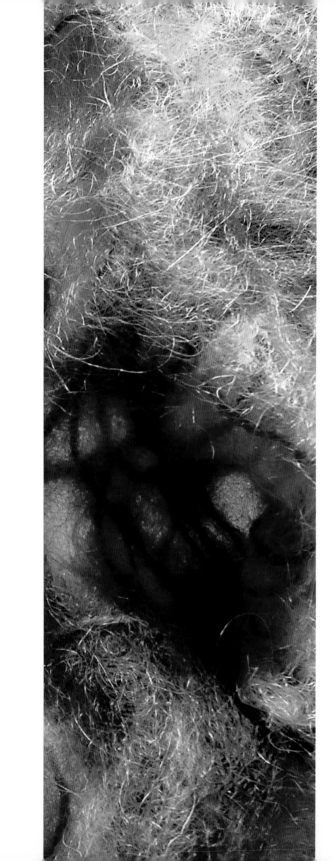

Why not take another look at the sky and begin again at the beginning? As you explore the ideas illustrated and begin to come up with discoveries and methods of your own, you'll learn how to take your textile creations to the next level. When it comes to designing with felt, the sky really is the limit...

Pages 300–305:
Three upside-down images of a stunning sunset over the Spanish Pyrenees, featuring altocumulus lenticularis and cirrus spissatus clouds.

Pages 310–311:
More images to inspire you to experiment with the techniques in this book.

Index of techniques

Some of the textiles illustrated in this book involve multiple techniques, to varying degrees. For simplicity's sake, only the principal techniques are listed here. It is also important to note that tufting and needle felting involve the same basic tools and methods but are worked from different sides of the support fabric.

Needle felting:

30–31, 48, 53, 61, 63, 65–66, 71, 77, 78, 109, 110, 114, 116, 119, 125, 126, 128, 142, 154 , 157, 158, 160, 165, 168, 172, 178, 185, 202, 212–213 , 218, 220, 233, 236, 250, 251, 253, 263, 273, 276, 277, 291, 297, 298, 299, 306

Ready-made felt and other fabrics:

87, 88–89, 90–91, 93, 97, 98–99, 101, 103, 104–105, 265, 268, 285, 286, 287, 289, 291

Tufting:

37, 57, 59, 80, 119, 127, 135, 138, 153, 204, 206, 242, 248, 252, 257, 272

Wet felting:

22–27, 43, 44, 46, 65–66, 71, 72, 84, 122, 123, 149, 151, 175, 176, 181, 188, 190, 193, 196, 201, 202, 208, 211, 216, 222, 226, 228, 261, 275, 279

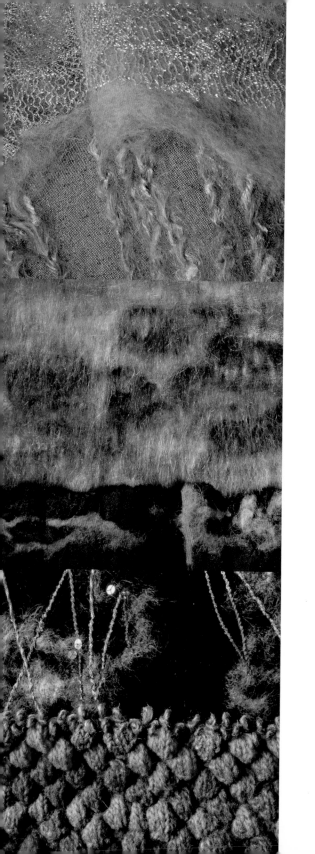

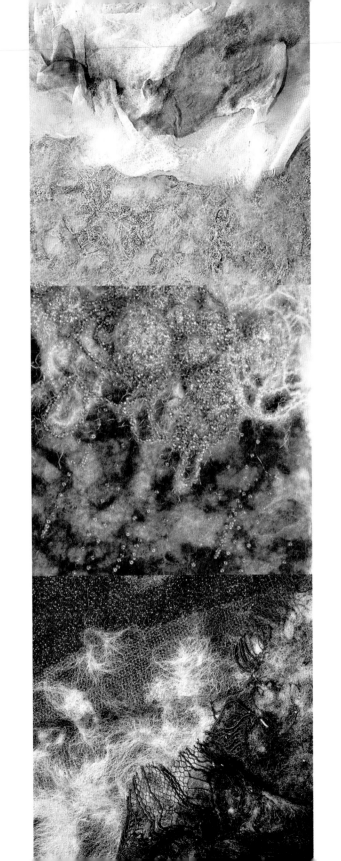

Acknowledgments

Many thanks to Marie-Hélène Nougier and all the team at Méteo-France in Roissy, especially Vincent Ducastin and Daniel Fournier, for their help and support.

Thanks also to Fred Lipka who gave me permission for my many visits to the felt factory in Mouzon, and also to the always warm and welcoming Jean Raulin, who, over the course of a year, showed me around and supplied me with all the information and samples I needed to understand the mysteries of industrial wet felting, needle felting and tufting. Thanks to the managers and staff at the Centre Tarkett Sommer in Sedan for their skill and warm welcome, and thanks also to everyone at the Musée du Feutre in Mouzon, which has just celebrated its twentieth anniversary.

I would also like to thank Jean Tellier and Christian Loumagne for their proofreading, and Odile Ouagne, Léa and Caroline Vernac for patiently acting as models.

Translated from the French *Feutres, regarder le ciel et créer.*

First published in the United Kingdom in 2008 by
Thames & Hudson Ltd, 181A High Holborn, London WC1V 7QX

www.thamesandhudson.com

First published in 2008 in paperback in the United States of America by
Thames & Hudson Inc., 500 Fifth Avenue, New York, New York 10110

thamesandhudsonusa.com

Original edition © 2007 Aubanel, an imprint of Éditions Minerva, Geneva
This edition © 2008 Thames & Hudson Ltd, London

British Library Cataloguing-in-Publication Data
A catalogue record for this book is available from the British Library

Library of Congress Catalog Card Number 2007905723

ISBN 978-0-500-28731-6

Printed in China